USING OFFSHORE HAVENS

FOR Privacy AND Profits

Using OFFSHORE HAVENS

for Privacy and Profits

ADAM STARCHILD

PALADIN PRESS
BOULDER, COLORADO

Also by Adam Starchild:

Keep What You Own: Protect Your Money, Property, and Family
   from Courts, Creditors, and the IRS
Portable Wealth: The Complete Guide to Precious Metals Investment
Protect Your Assets: How to Avoid Falling Victim to the
   Government's Forfeiture Laws
Reviving the American Dream: Stop "Just Getting By" and Build Real Wealth
Swiss Money Secrets: How You Can Legally Hide Your Money in Switzerland

Using Offshore Havens for Privacy and Profits
by Adam Starchild

Copyright © 1994 by Adam Starchild

ISBN 0-87364-767-X
Printed in the United States of America

Published by Paladin Press, a division of
Paladin Enterprises, Inc., P.O. Box 1307,
Boulder, Colorado 80306, USA.
(303) 443-7250

Direct inquiries and/or orders to the above address.

PALADIN, PALADIN PRESS, and the "horse head" design
are trademarks belonging to Paladin Enterprises and
registered in the United States Patent and Trademark Office.

All rights reserved. Except for use in a review, no
portion of this book may be reproduced in any form
without the express written permission of the publisher.

Neither the author nor the publisher assumes
any responsibility for the use or misuse of
information contained in this book.

CONTENTS

Introduction
    The Case for Investing Abroad   1

Chapter 1
    Forfeitures and Lawsuits   11

Chapter 2
    Get Your Wealth Out Before Exchange Controls   21

Chapter 3
    Of Morality and Patriotism   23

Chapter 4
    Using the Offshore Bank Account Loophole   27

Chapter 5
    Naive Fools Spend Time in Prison   41

Chapter 6
    Prudent Ways for Americans to Buy Offshore Funds   45

Chapter 7
    Great Britain   49

Chapter 8
    The British Isles   65

Chapter 9
    The Cayman Islands   77

Chapter 10
    Hong Kong   85

Chapter 11 Switzerland	89
Chapter 12 Liechtenstein	111
Chapter 13 Luxembourg	119
Chapter 14 Austria	129
Chapter 15 The Use of Tax Havens	137
Chapter 16 The Money Laundry under Attack	141
Conclusion	151

INTRODUCTION: THE CASE FOR INVESTING ABROAD

Why invest abroad? Isn't the United States still the most stable, free, and prosperous nation on earth? What safer haven could I possibly find for my assets? Where else could I find such a diverse range of investment opportunity?

Today the economic outlook is bleak. The cyclical disinflation of recent years should not obscure the inevitability of resurgent inflation, the result of the staggering budget deficits, and the monetization of this debt through expansionist Federal Reserve policies.

To all of this, politicians of whatever party or ideological perspective will respond in the same predictable manner. First, they will enact exchange controls to prevent assets from moving to a safer, more inflation-proof country or currency. Then, with private wealth frozen within the country, they will embark on an orgy of taxation and confiscation measures against the hostage assets in a vain effort to bail out the bankrupt federal budget process.

This describes precisely the sequence of events during the last great U.S. inflation and in virtually every nation of the world that has ever suffered hyperinflation. To assume that it cannot or will not happen again is to ignore all the evidence of history.

What then can we do about it? Political solutions cannot and will not work because inflationary policies are a consequence of government's natural antagonism to private capital. Politicians will never adopt noninflationary policies because it is not in their perceived self-interest to do so. As bad as it is, inflation has always been the easy way out for the politicians. There is only one practical solution open to independent investors: get a portion of your wealth safely diversified abroad, while you can.

Many investors feel unsure about putting some of their money in a foreign country. All things being equal between nations, there really would be no reason to diversify your investments internationally. After all, you know your own country much better than any other. You know your laws, your customs, and the people with whom you deal habitually, while foreign customs seem to be strange indeed. If you keep your assets in your own country, it is much easier to keep an eye on them and to get to them rapidly when they are needed.

But all things are not equal between nations. Some currencies are traditionally stronger and more inflation free than others. Interest rates vary, as do foreign-exchange regulations, banking laws, securities regulations, and political and economic freedom. Therefore, geographical diversification has become necessary for prudent investors of any nationality—even for the Swiss.

Most nations of the world eagerly welcome foreign capital, offering tax advantages and favorable interest and exchange rates to woo investors' capital from other nations.

Sending a portion of your capital outside your own nation requires that you sharpen your awareness of a whole new set of economic and political indicators. Each nation has different regulations, taxes, and exchange restrictions, not to mention the limitations on personal freedoms of speech, assembly, religion, and petition of grievances. It makes sense to compare nations as carefully as you compare brokers, bankers, bond ratings, or any other investment you make.

The Case for Investing Abroad

For many, it makes sense to have some of their assets in another government jurisdiction to hedge against political trends in their own nation. That way, they can watch events at home unfold with the security of knowing that at least some of their property is outside the reach of their own government's greedy hands.

In 1928, U.S. Supreme Court Justice Louis Brandeis wrote that "the right to be let alone is the most comprehensive of rights and the right most valued by civilized men" (Olmstead v. United States). The irony of that statement is that Justice Brandeis was writing a minority opinion in the case, and his opinion has been in the minority among bureaucrats and politicians ever since. In the Olmstead case, the 5-to-4 majority gave the FBI permission to wiretap suspected gangsters, and such wiretapping is now widely considered to be a legitimate activity of government agencies. Let a little government in the door and you get a lot of government intervention down the line.

By 1971, with the passage of the grossly misnamed Bank Secrecy Act in the United States, government access to private banking transactions became almost total. This law commands banks, among other things, to microfilm all checks of more than $100. The Bank Secrecy Act actually wipes out any pretense of privacy in banking transactions. The government has virtually deputized the banker to enforce federal policies instead of the customer's wishes.

In the United States, our financial lives have become totally transparent to the government. Notice how often you are asked for your Social Security number, even for nonfinancial applications. When you apply for any kind of loan or credit application, notice the breadth and depth of information that goes on your record—some of it having nothing to do with finances. On your Internal Revenue Service (IRS) 1040 form each April, notice the information being requested in detail. A complex return may include 10 or more pages of special schedules, listings of all companies paying you dividends, all banks paying you interest, etc. It seems the government doesn't just want our money; it wants to know every detail of our lives.

This financial information is kept in public and private files all over the nation. The IRS computer has every detail of your tax forms from over the years. The private credit files contain all the information you put on loan or insurance applications (e.g., health history). All your former employers have files on you. You would be amazed at the paper trail you have created by a lifetime of filling out forms.

Back in 1928, when Justice Brandeis eloquently expressed what the majority of Americans (if not justices) believed, there was a great heritage of privacy and independence in America. People did not share personal or financial information with their neighbors, or even their children. "Silent Cal" Coolidge was president, and he exemplified the closed-mouth Yankee virtue of silence when he said, "I've never been hurt by anything I didn't say." And that says a lot.

Today, it is not uncommon to hear light cocktail banter about how much an investor has in T-bills, Swiss francs, bonds, etc., or to brag about one's "secret Swiss bank account" to a near-stranger, who just might be an undercover federal agent or informer! We often hear people divulge their salary and outside income to anyone who asks or broadcast the value of their real estate, cars, or other possessions. The virtue of holding financial information in confidence has apparently been eroded badly since the days of Silent Cal.

In his novel *Cancer Ward*, Alexander Solzhenitsyn uses an interesting imagery about what government reporting looks (and feels) like: "As every man goes through life," he writes, "he fills in a number of forms for the record, each containing a number of questions. There are thus hundreds of little threads radiating from every man, millions of threads in all, and if these threads were to suddenly become visible, the whole sky would look like a spider's web. They are not visible, they are not material, but every man is constantly aware of their existence."

It is possible to begin cutting away some of those threads

The Case for Investing Abroad

or, at the very least, to limit the number of new informational threads being attached to us. We can first of all begin giving out less information about ourselves. It's possible to conduct financial matters without using checking accounts, which are microfilmed, or credit cards. You can use cashier's checks, traveler's checks, money orders, or cash. There are many ways to keep your financial affairs more private.

Second, we can conduct at least a portion of our banking and investment activity in a land that respects our financial privacy. If you compare the practices of your U.S. bankers to the practices of offshore bankers, it will become obvious to you that foreign bankers respect your money and your privacy, while their U.S. counterparts usually do not. Investors who overlook the stocks of overseas companies may be missing two-thirds of their opportunities.

U.S. issues represent little more than one-third of the world's total market in stock issues. And growth moves around. It was in Japan; now it is in Taiwan, Singapore, South Korea; in the future it will be in Thailand, even Vietnam. And don't overlook Latin America.

Mutual funds offer an easy way for investors to get involved in the stocks of foreign companies. So-called international funds invest solely in foreign companies; global funds mix in U.S. stocks. And increasingly, the funds are focusing on specific countries or regions, such as Southeast Asia.

Investors can also buy pieces of the foreign companies directly, through American Depository Receipts (ADRs), which are traded on U.S. stock exchanges. ADRs, which represent shares of a foreign stock, are issued by U.S. banks that take possession of the securities. The banks convert dividend payments into dollars for ADR holders and deduct foreign withholding taxes.

ADRs give international investors a little more guarantee because those foreign companies have to meet certain accounting standards. For example, German companies that made only limited disclosures have to provide more information when moving into the U.S. markets.

Some investors dismiss investments in overseas companies as risky, but many of them are more conservative than their U.S. counterparts. For example, Swiss drug stocks typically have a price-to-earnings ratio of less than half that of U.S. companies. (Dividing a share's price by the company's earnings per share is a basic way to compare stock prices.)

Think of brand names known worldwide for investment potential. Companies such as Coca-Cola, Boeing, Disney, Ford, Citicorp, and Philip Morris are so multinational that they are not dependent on the U.S. economy, which is one of the things an investor would like to achieve.

There are good foreign bonds, too; it just takes more research to invest in suitable bonds.

Global investors must be patient. People invest in real estate and hold it for 10 or 15 years without thinking anything of it, but in stocks they often expect instant results.

Today there is a large and violent dependent population whose members demand that politicians protect them from falling living standards. But governments cannot fulfill this expectation. They are more bankrupt than ever before and likely to become more so. The impact of information technology will result in tens of millions of low-skilled service workers being made redundant in the next few years. This will lead to a further shortfall in tax revenues and more demands upon politicians to redistribute income from an empty pocket.

A crisis looms ahead. Desperate for money, politicians will raise taxes, impose exchange controls, and institute other policies designed to confiscate wealth wherever they find it. No doubt, they will attempt to dilute the value of your capital through inflation. And as investors turn to gold as a protection against inflation, you can expect history to repeat itself. Authorities in the United States confiscated private gold holdings in the depression of the 1930s. They may seek to do so again in the depression of the 1990s.

Now, with the Clinton administration, we have both a president and a Congress who firmly believe in the redistri-

The Case for Investing Abroad

bution of wealth as a social goal. It is important to keep in mind that these goals and attitudes are going to be with us throughout the Clinton administration—it is not enough just to focus on whatever proposals might currently be pending. Already in the debates on the various estate-tax proposals, members of Congress are being heard to say things like "people shouldn't be allowed to take it with them—it must be distributed to society."

Having some of your assets offshore will also provide a degree of protection against creditors and lawsuits. While this is not as complete as setting up an irrevocable trust, it does provide you with some advantages. By the time a claimant receives the proper authority to access your assets, you could have the account moved to another jurisdiction. The claimant may give up on those assets rather than continue to chase them.

To quote Harry Browne: "Never keep all your wealth in the country where you live. Keep part of your assets hidden and beyond the government's reach." Only then, he writes, will you "know you own something, somewhere, that the government isn't going to get its hands on." (Harry Browne is the author of a number of books on investing and was one of the pioneers of encouraging Americans to invest internationally.)

We can't claim to know exactly what nasty surprises the government has in store for us next, but Doug Casey—the editor of *Crisis Investing* newsletter and the author of several books on investment—put it very well when he said that "one of the fixed points in the cosmos is the stupidity and malevolence of government."

It has been hard enough to convince individuals to look outside the conventional investment media of stocks, bonds, and life insurance for financial safety, but the idea that it might also be necessary for them to look outside the borders of the United States for capital protection is more than most can comprehend.

The reluctance of Americans to consider investing abroad is a natural consequence of their heritage. The U.S. dollar was the strongest currency in the world during most of this century. America had a long history of protecting the property of individual citizens. The revolutions and wars that laid waste to other nations and destroyed the savings and investments of their citizens barely touched American shores.

And most important of all, for the first 150 years of American history, the individual was able to keep the major part of whatever he earned, either from his business or from his investments, without fear that the state would confiscate his gains. In total freedom, he could move his capital in and out of the country without the permission of government. In other words, the American investor kept his investment in his own country because of both the opportunities and the safety.

Today, growing numbers of investors are convinced that the United States is no longer the land of safety or opportunity. A few of the more astute investors are shedding their resistance to the idea of having their wealth kept thousands of miles away, across oceans and borders. There is a growing flight of U.S. capital abroad. But still, up until now, only the most adventurous of U.S. investors has actually taken the time and effort to look into the opportunities abroad. The great majority remain ignorant of both the reasons for needing to take their capital out of the country and the market mechanisms by which they can do it.

There are many countries today that fight their own domestic economic problems by holding their citizens' wealth hostage. The battle by citizens to evade these restrictions is documented by occasional news stories of important people being caught in the act of "smuggling" their own money across borders.

But just as citizens export their wealth to avoid its confiscation, so governments work diligently to close the escape routes. Foreign exchange controls, currency controls, credit controls, and taxes on foreign holdings are devices created by the politicians to either freeze wealth within their jurisdiction (so they can confiscate it when ready) or to discourage people from bothering to take it abroad. As the flight of capital continues, even in the face of these laws, the laws are tightened, the severity of the penalties for capital export are increased, and the propaganda machine of government is turned on fully against the "rich" speculators who are escaping with assets that "should rightly belong to the nation."

Escaping the net of the government is not the only reason you might want to place funds outside the country. There are certainly other legitimate benefits from such actions.

For instance, there might be investment opportunities available abroad that aren't available in the United States. While U.S. real estate may be overpriced because of intensive government subsidy and intervention, comparable real estate in other markets is often selling at bargain-basement rates. World stock markets do not move in tandem; when the U.S. market is languishing, others may be booming. While savings accounts in U.S. banks may be guaranteed losers as the dollar depreciates, savings accounts in selected currencies in other countries consistently maintain their purchasing power.

Whatever happens, you want to be prepared in advance, and capital preservation through international diversification is a superb hedge against any contingency. The knowledge that a portion of your wealth is waiting for you, where nobody but you can touch it, creates a sense of security and a freedom from fear. That's something you can't put a price tag on.

CHAPTER 1

FORFEITURES AND LAWSUITS

In the past it was the practice in this country that when a person wished to retain a lawyer to sue someone that he or she would pay the lawyer a fee, and the lawyer would examine the issues and then would proceed based on the merits of the case. This is no longer the case.

Due to the contingency system, we now have lawsuits being filed at the rate of one hundred million cases a year. Many of these suits have nothing to do with right and wrong, but, instead, are predicated on the desire of one party to extract wealth from another party. In many cases, this equation is not based on the desire to extract real wealth, but rather on a desire to extract small payments as "nuisance" settlements because it is cheaper to pay the money than to fight the suit.

If this was not bad enough, it is also a problem for those who are not sued, because another part of the problem becomes the cost to the taxpayers of maintaining the court system to handle this litigation.

If we assume that one is lucky enough to make it through the legal maze without becoming a target, then at time of death the federal government under today's law would take roughly 50 percent of a family's wealth as the transfer is made from mother and father to children of all amounts over

$1.2 million. Several bills have proposed even more onerous taxation.

If you have attempted to pursue the American dream of wealth, of independence, have the ability to control your life, you may very well be disappointed by these facts. In fact, you may be frightened. You may be, for the first time in your life, considering leaving the country. According to *Money* magazine, at least 250,000 people per year move out of the United States.

For many people the threshold issue in moving assets offshore for protection is "do I need it?" Many people believe this won't happen to me, it can't happen to my business, my family is safe, because we don't do anything that's dangerous. The reality of life in America is that you don't have to do anything dangerous; all you really have to do is be in the wrong place at the wrong time. Ordinary people have extraordinary problems. In many cases these problems are not problems of their own doing; they are simply matters of circumstance.

Imagine a group of business partners getting together for an informal lunch to discuss their work, one of the secretarial staff in the office is asked to go to a local restaurant and pick up an order for these partners. Unbeknownst to the partners as part of her normal work environment, this secretary has a poor driving record, several accidents and speeding are the main cause of these problems. The secretary leaves the building, climbs into their car, and proceeds to pick up lunch. In the midst of this trip excessive speed is taken by the employee. The employee pays more attention to the radio than to an upcoming stop sign. The stop sign is run, a car is smashed, a life is lost. A subsequent lawsuit, one would think, would simply blame the employee for her negligence, but unfortunately this is not the case.

All of the partners are sued as the result of their negligence in not determining that this driver was in fact unsafe. More importantly, this driver was on company business, and the heirs of the life that was lost now seek retribution from the remaining partners. Their homes, their college funds, their boats, their vacation homes, even their business are up for grabs.

In many cases one of the prime financial elements that is being sought is insurance. In days gone by, insurance was a protector of the family and the business. Nowadays it often acts as a target.

CIVIL ASSET FORFEITURE: THE RISK PEOPLE DON'T WANT TO TALK ABOUT

Forfeiture is even more difficult to protect against than lawsuits. For this reason, many people feel that domestic lawsuit protection strategies are inadequate, because as long as the assets are located in the United States, they can be forfeited, regardless of trusts, partnerships, or other ways of titling the assets that may protect them from ordinary lawsuits.

Any property-owning U.S. citizen, and any investor with property located in the United States, must become knowledgeable about the threat of civil asset forfeiture—government's police power to confiscate your real and personal property, based on that property's alleged use or involvement in criminal activities.

The threat of government confiscation applies to homeowners, landlords, people with a resort condo, investors or partners in hotels, restaurants and bars and those who own farm or undeveloped land. Even retail business and commercial property owners are at serious risk.

For people concerned about protecting their wealth, particularly real estate, avoidance of potential asset forfeiture is a compelling reason to take careful preventive action—or to avoid certain types of real estate investments completely. Avoidance of civil asset forfeiture is not an easy task, especially because of investor complacency based on a traditional belief in a host of U.S. constitutional safeguards for private property ownership. Alarmingly, many of these former legal protections have collapsed under the pressure of a growing American police state.

Civil asset forfeiture laws are being enforced with Gestapo-like zeal by state and federal police authorities and courts in a highly unjust manner. These questionable official acts, literally robbing private citizens, depend for their dubious authority on a combination of musty legal doctrines dating back to early English common law, and the eagerness of contemporary politicians to "get tough" on crime and drugs, even at the expense of personal liberty.

A standard legal dictionary definition of "forfeiture" (until a few years ago), would have been the "loss of some right or property as a penalty for some illegal act." Whether you call it forfeiture, confiscation, expropriation or commandeering, it all amounts to the same thing: government now has the arbitrary power to seize almost any privately-owned property. Property is in danger of seizure if it was 1) *allegedly* purchased with the proceeds of illegal activity; 2) *allegedly* used to "facilitate" criminal activity, or 3) *alleged* to be the location of criminal activity.

The word "alleged" is emphasized because the statutory and judicial procedures governing forfeitures allow police to seize your property, *prior* to any hearing before a judge or magistrate, and to keep the property without charging you with any crime. They have the right to retain it until *you* are able to prove your property is not tainted by criminal conduct.

Much of what you may have learned in the past about your guaranteed rights and liberties no longer applies to property rights. Increased government and police powers, the perception of rising criminal activity and violence, popular anxiety about drug use—all these were the political justifications for curtailing the application of the Bill of Rights and the individual security it once guaranteed. Police and government agents now have the power to seize your business, home, bank account, records, and personal property, all without prior indictment, hearing, or trial. Everything you possess can be taken away at the whim of one or two state

Forfeitures and Lawsuits 15

or federal officials who may target you secretly. Regardless of sex, age, race, or economic status, we are all just a knock on the door away from becoming potential victims of civil asset forfeiture and its abuse.

Lest you believe the mistaken notion that asset forfeiture only concerns drug-related crimes, you should know there are now more than 100 different federal forfeiture statutes, addressing a wide range of illegal conduct, both criminal and civil.

Some of the federal government agencies with statutory forfeiture power include the Drug Enforcement Administration and the U.S. Customs Bureau of the Treasury Department, the Federal Bureau of Investigation, U.S. Coast Guard, the U.S. Postal Service, the Bureau of Land Management and the Fish and Wildlife Bureau (both in the Interior Department), the Securities and Exchange Commission, the Department of Health and Human Services, the Food and Drug Administration, the Justice Department (including the Immigration and Naturalization Service), the Department of Housing and Urban Development, and, of course, the Internal Revenue Service—plus more than 3,000 state and local police departments.

New Jersey is a state with one of the most severe forfeiture laws, triggered by *any* alleged criminal conduct, even shoplifting. That statute denies the right to a trial by jury on the issue of forfeiture. Its application is so severe that a male gynecologist, Owen A. Chang, M.D., accused of conducting a medical exam of a female patient without the presence of a nurse, as required by local law, had his office equipment and building confiscated. Kathy Schrama, accused of stealing UPS packages worth at most $500 from her neighbors' doorsteps in New Jersey, saw local police take away her home, two cars and all her furniture—even the Christmas presents she had purchased for her 10-year-old son. A building contractor who bid on, received, properly executed, and was paid for several construction contracts for New Jersey municipalities later had his entire business confiscated by the state based on an allegation that his company was not legally qualified to make the bids in the first place.

Arizona's statutes are also an example of the trend in abandoning any distinction between civil and criminal forfeiture, applying unlimited forfeiture with few procedural protections for property owners as a handy supplement to criminal law enforcement. The state's assistant attorney general, Cameron Holmes, proudly describes his state's law as "a stride in the evolution of a 'civil justice system' to complement the 'criminal justice system' through judicial intervention in antisocial behavior." This is the sort of exceedingly fuzzy thinking which has served to expand property confiscation and shrink personal legal protection and freedom.

Not content with applying forfeiture law to drug offenses, legislators and prosecutors are rapidly expanding the forfeiture principle to cover a host of alleged criminal acts in every area of activity. A growing number of states, including Texas, New Jersey, and Florida, now apply civil forfeiture to *any* criminal activity, which means owners must police their real property against all criminal activity or possibly lose it. Homeowners and landlords are being forced into the role not only of "their brother's keeper," but held responsible for the acts of their children, spouse, guests, and tenants—and even their tenant's guests.

Make a mistake on a loan application and you may face forfeiture. In an attempt to curb savings and loan fraud, in 1989 Congress made it a criminal offense to give false information on a loan application. Now this law is being used by the government to confiscate the property financed with loan proceeds, even years later, and even if all payments are up to date. Under this loan application law, in Florida in 1991, the U.S. Marshal's Service seized $11 million worth of commercial property including five convenience stores, a multiplex movie theater, and a consumer electronics store.

To give you an idea of how far this has gone, in 1993 a federal circuit court ruled that defendants charged with illegally modifying, selling, and using television signal

Forfeitures and Lawsuits 17

"descramblers" (which allow satellite dishes to pick up coded TV signals) were violating federal wiretapping laws. Such acts are not only felonies but forfeitable crimes, meaning your house could be taken away if you install a TV signal descrambler.

These forfeiture laws are little known, and although these examples show how widely they are used, most people tend to brush off the news and think, "well, they must have done something." None of this information is that hard to find—much of it is published in required legal notices of the forfeitures in daily newspapers, but people just don't pay attention to its significance—until it is too late and it is their property being seized. *Time* and *Newsweek* have covered these stories frequently—and were the source of many of the incidents listed here. You had a chance to read them too. Did you? And did you think about it? (Although a number of cases have been given as examples, the final outcomes may vary through litigation, which often takes years, so the final results may not be the same as given at the time of writing.)

As you begin to see, the possibilities of you and your property being ensnared by government forfeiture are endless.

SOURCES OF HELP

This book does not offer a do-it-yourself kit of forms to finalize incorporation abroad. Such a quicky deal is as dangerous as performing a kidney operation on your own wife by using a do-it-yourself surgical manual. The manual may be all right, but who in his right mind would risk it? In principle, a "Do-It-Yourself Offshore Havens Manual" is possible; whatever expertise professionals have in the field could be formulated in precise and complete detail. However, such a book, if honestly and competently put together, would be gigantic, and would amount to a combination of relevant legal training, relevant accountancy training, and much more detailed information about the tax and corporate laws of a multitude of countries. The time required for a layman to digest such a manual would be worth more than the price of good professional advice. Trying to avoid both such a detailed manual and the costs of professional advice, using a shortcut approach, would be cheaper in the short run—and much, much more costly in the long run.

So anyone interested in pursuing any of the possibilities presented here should definitely get in touch with the best professional advisors he can afford before going into action. It will mean risks, expense, and hard work, but properly done, it could be very much worth it.

One of the best sources of help in setting up offshore trusts and corporations is an American certified accountant who has a large practice in Panama. Marc Harris holds a master's degree in business administration from Columbia University in New York, and completed the certified public accountancy examination at the age of 18. He is believed to be the youngest person in the United States to pass the examination.

He opened his Panamanian firm in 1985, after being a consultant with the accounting firm of Ernst & Whinney. His services are highly recommended because he is able to create and administer offshore corporations and trusts with complete compliance with U.S. laws. Often an American client uses a tax-haven based advisor who knows the local laws but is not familiar with American tax law requirements and technicalities, and the client eventually gets into trouble, so Marc Harris has a unique ability to bridge the two worlds for his clients. Although based in Panama, he can create and administer corporations and trusts that are registered in all of the popular tax havens. This tends to lower the cost, since the administrative work is being done in lower-cost Panama. It also provides the protection of two sets of secrecy laws—the site of incorporation, and the site of the accounting records—putting a series of hurdles in the path of anyone seeking information.

For more information, write to The Harris Organization, Attn: Traditional Client Services, Estafeta El Dorado, Apartado Postal 6-1097, Panama 6, Panama.

For those who prefer to have U.S.-based help, Asset Protection Corporation is a management team of lawyers, investment advisors, and accountants, which works with lawyers (as well as directly with clients) throughout the country. They will send a free information package on request. For information contact Asset Protection Corporation, Suite 201A, 14418 Old Mill Road, Upper Marlboro, Maryland 20772. This source can also help with domestic strategies, such as family limited partnerships, limited liability companies, and trusts.

INVEST WISELY

One of the oft neglected areas of the investment of an American's money in an offshore environment is what the actual investment scenario will be. Many times Americans enter a world in which they are unfamiliar and do not recognize the significant risks that can be made in investing in a world where issues of bonds, stocks, annuities, CDs, etc., are done in an unpredictable and unknown environment.

It is imperative that domestic investors be aware of the risks that they are taking and the market conditions they are entering. More times than not, what the less than professional investor should be doing is seeking professional and accredited money management. If one were to turn to organizations like Jardine-Fleming in Hong Kong, Asset Protection Corporation in the United States, JML Swiss Investment Counsellors in Switzerland, or The Harris Organization in Panama, many times the unwieldy and unknown aspects of international investment would become easy and routine to deal with.

A decade or two ago, tax haven countries were used primarily by wealthy families setting up trusts for the grandchildren. As tax laws have changed, such simple solutions are generally no longer possible.

But today the same countries are being used, with the same trust and corporate forms, to provide asset protection. The tax neutrality of the tax haven countries is ideal for this purpose, since there is no additional tax complication for the person seeking asset protection. Thus the tax haven business has slowly evolved into the asset protection business.

It is preferable by far to stay with jurisdictions where the asset protection features have evolved as a fundamental part of the law and the local social and political structure. The Swiss law protecting insurance policies from seizure has been in effect since 1908—not to attract foreign business but because the Swiss wanted it to protect themselves. A Swiss court isn't going to look for excuses to carve exceptions out of the law.

Panama has been a corporate management center since it became a country, because that business was an integral part of the commercial center that developed around the Panama Canal.

Using offshore havens is an art, not a science, which means that you will find contradictions in this book. One of the things to bear in mind when studying an art is that taste plays a role. The offshore strategy that suits the needs, and prejudices, of one person may not suit those of another. It is not an exact science that can be replicated through experiments and demonstrations.

Some may want to use a U.S. asset protection firm to implement a carefully structured asset protection plan combining tax, investment, and estate planning, while gaining asset protection as part of the package. Others may decide to go directly offshore, perhaps purchasing a Swiss annuity and forming a British Virgin Islands corporation managed from Panama, without seeking U.S. planning and legal advice.

Most of these decisions are somewhat subjective, and depend upon your personality and your personal experience as much as they do on law. You have to go with the people, countries, and cultures that you feel comfortable with.

People frequently ask what is the best offshore haven, or what is the best country in which to open a bank account. There is no "best" answer—these things are very subjective and depend upon what you want to do.

CHAPTER 2

GET YOUR WEALTH OUT BEFORE EXCHANGE CONTROLS

When exchange controls take effect in any country, there is no warning. Most people don't realize that the United States already has such legislation on the books, ready for implementation by the president through executive order at any time. The International Emergency Economic Powers Act (Title II of Public Law 95-223) is a little-known act passed in 1977 without fanfare during the week between Christmas and New Year's. It gives the president complete power to "prohibit any transactions in foreign exchange," including "the importing or exporting of currency and securities" (Section 203a), in order "to deal with any unusual and extraordinary threat, which has its source in whole or substantial part outside the United States." (Section 202a). This act thus could prohibit all exchanges of currency, even wire transfers to other countries.

It has already been used by every president since it was passed. Carter used it against Iran, Reagan against Russia, and Bush against Iraq. But it could easily be used against any and all countries.

The growth of American investors' interest in global and international mutual funds is popularizing foreign investments in ways that may invoke such controls. And these U.S.-based mutual funds are the very ones that are most vulnerable to controls, since they hold the money for tens of thousands of individual investors. In the right circumstances, it would not even be that difficult to order these funds to be liquidated and repatriate foreign holdings—an edict that would be difficult or impossible to enforce against individual investors with direct foreign investments.

Another forgotten law on the books is the Interest Equalization Tax Act. There is no reason for it to have been forgotten, but most investors (and most Americans) seem to have conveniently short memories. It is only 20 years since gold was legal for Americans to own, and the same length of time since the Interest Equalization Tax was lowered to zero. And that is the key—it was lowered to a temporary zero rate, not abolished or repealed. First enacted in 1964, it put a 15-percent tax on all purchases of foreign securities. It could be raised again at any time, and this time it would also affect all purchases of U.S. mutual funds investing internationally. These did not exist in 1964, but they do now—and are very vulnerable. Such a tax would not affect their existing holdings, but what happens to a fund that can only hold its existing securities and cannot replace them with other foreign securities? The whole management aspect of the fund is destroyed, and management is what you are paying a mutual fund to do for you. And the inability to manage would be likely to cause a run on all these funds, with forced liquidations to meet redemptions causing distress sales of portfolio holdings—or a suspension of redemptions.

CHAPTER 3
OF MORALITY AND PATRIOTISM

Should you support the government's efforts to keep your money within its borders on the basis that it is patriotic, good for the nation, ethical, or moral?

First, it is imperative that we establish exactly the purposes of international diversification of your assets and the political implications. This book examines a highly effective method of asset protection and growth. But who really wants to protect his assets and reduce his taxes? The question may seem stupidly naive. Who doesn't want to keep more of what's his? But this sort of answer, derived from the cynical "everyone is selfish" notion, is not what we are looking for.

Asset protection through the use of international financial strategies and diversification requires considerable initiative, alertness, determination, and dedication. Not that it doesn't pay. Sad to say, the net gain from each hour dedicated to protecting your wealth is almost certain to be higher than the net gain from an hour of productive employment. Thanks to "progressive" taxation, this goes double for someone in a relatively high tax bracket. There is also a psychological dimension that must not be neglected. Most people derive a "clean" feeling from making a living through their work but feel that there is something dirty about scheming to reduce their taxes.

Heavy taxes, whether used to provide luxury for a ruling elite or to support welfare schemes, always have the effect of penalizing individual initiative and productivity, reducing investment capital and thus the resources required for economic growth, reducing the standard of living, and forcing individuals to hide things, both activities and incomes, from the government and from one another. Heavy taxation is, therefore, a danger to the future of the high-tax countries.

Internationalizing assets assumes at the outset that the investor has assets that are available for investment. It also assumes that a viable means of doing so exists in the contemporary scheme of world business and, ideally, that a plan exists that includes short- and long-range investment goals.

To consider the question of the morality of diversification and tax avoidance, it is first necessary to set forth a working definition of the word morality. In the context of taxation, morality is not considered an absolute, but a concept that, like the tax laws themselves, is subject to interpretation. One person might argue quite convincingly that it is morally wrong to tax a working widow with children to help provide the day-to-day support for a war veteran who is able to work but prefers not to; another person can argue just as convincingly on behalf of the veteran. Others would argue the libertarian position that all taxation is theft.

The morality of taxation changes with the times. Prior to World War I, when taxes were comparatively low, though certainly not popular, most workers and small businessmen were exempt from the controversy by virtue of low incomes. During times of national emergency, particularly during and directly following World War II, tax avoidance was frowned upon even by those who were looking at larger tax liabilities each year. But as progressive tax rates brought taxes higher and higher each year in highly industrialized and populated nations, the attitudes of taxpayers underwent a gradual but definitive change.

Today, even the individual worker for whom the tax system is supposedly designed can see that a tax system in which higher-income brackets produce progressively higher tax rates is stultifying to individual initiative and productivity. Investors feel not only duty-bound but morally obligated to use the legal tax avoidance measures available to them. Whether the tax loss to the nation is through using domestic tax shelter strategies or through the use of an international financial center, the avoidance principle is exactly the same. From a purely pragmatic viewpoint, legal tax avoidance by an investor may not be the road to wealth but simply a means of economic survival for himself and his family.

The losers in this business of tax avoidance are presumed to be the heavily industrialized, heavily populated, and heavily taxed countries of the world. If two nations could personify this description, they would be the United States and Great Britain. Yet the attitudes of these governments toward tax avoidance is ambivalent to say the least. The United States, for example, actually established itself as a tax haven for foreigners by not imposing a withholding tax on interest paid to foreigners on their U.S. bank deposits and allowing foreigners to buy, hold, and sell U.S. securities without incurring a capital gains liability.

There are, of course, economic reasons to justify these tax rulings (a reversal of the ruling on interest paid on bank deposits would remove billions of dollars from U.S. banks). This being the case, we can say that there is no external threat to tax avoidance from free world nations. The United States and Switzerland are both involved in the business of providing a haven for foreign investors to protect their assets. The citizens of each frequently use the other for international diversification, and neither is likely to try to put the other out of business.

The arguments that apply to taxation apply even more strongly to asset preservation through international diversification. Much of the growth in China today is being funded by Chinese investors in Hong Kong who got their capital out of China during the Communist takeover and are now providing the funds to restore capitalism to their country.

Preservation of wealth often involves a timely decision to move capital from one place, or one form, to another. Many times capital would have been lost if it had not been wisely redeployed as circumstances changed. Capital is always under political threat when it is in a minority. The periods of greatest risk are times of public disorder when many are impoverished and only a few are wise enough or lucky enough to preserve their wealth.

In 1931, Britain went off the gold standard. At that time, investments in gold coins could be bought for £100, which would now sell for £50,000, while government bonds could be bought for £100 and would now sell for £30. Yet in 1931, government bonds were thought a safer investment than gold coins and were the only investments allowed for most trustees.

This shows how families can rapidly be reduced from prosperity to poverty. The difference between two investments in one lifetime could easily amount to one investment rising 12 times as fast as inflation while the other falls to no more than 1 percent of its original purchasing power. Take the experience of what happened in one generation in Britain as a likely model for what lies ahead for North America.

The government destroys capital. Allowing it to destroy yours is not a rational path to prosperity or security. To whatever extent it is successful, production falls. The more you feed the crocodile, the bigger it grows.

The one clear answer is self-protection. But how? The rest of this book will show that there are ways—very elegant solutions that are completely legal and risk free.

CHAPTER 4
USING THE OFFSHORE BANK ACCOUNT LOOPHOLE

A key to taking advantage of offshore secrecy havens is the offshore bank account. It can be used as part of an aggressive wealth-building strategy or a defensive wealth-preservation and asset-protection plan. It was not many years ago that a person needed to be wealthy to benefit from an offshore bank account. But international banking and communications have changed dramatically. The offshore bank account is now a quick, inexpensive entry to foreign investment opportunities and other benefits.

Offshore bank accounts inspire many images in people's minds. There are visions of international drug dealers laundering billions of dollars in drug profits through Panamanian, Bahamian, and other offshore banks. Others think of the CIA setting up front organizations for its operations and using offshore accounts to pay for expenses, informants, and operatives. Offshore bank accounts have been used to conceal bribes paid to foreign officials, even royalty. The Iran-Contra operation allegedly involved the extensive use of foreign bank accounts.

Although these images and stories make for good reading, they have little to do with our present purposes, which are to make money and to protect our assets. The offshore bank account is a highly effective and economic way to achieve those goals.

USES OF THE OFFSHORE BANK ACCOUNT

The offshore bank account allows you to invest in foreign stocks and mutual funds that are not registered with U.S. government agencies. The account also might carry transaction costs lower than those of other methods.

An offshore bank account offers more options than most U.S. accounts. You can use the account as a way to profit from currency fluctuations, buy stocks or mutual funds, purchase foreign real estate, and earn the high interest rates available in many foreign countries. You also can trade precious metals and other assets through most foreign accounts.

The offshore bank account also provides a measure of asset protection. The existence of the offshore account will not readily be known by someone seeking to collect against your assets. The account probably will be revealed in your tax returns, and you will be legally obliged to include it in any required statement of your assets. But the creditor will have to file a separate court action and get a separate judgment in the country in which the account is located. This will allow you time to fight the action or simply move the assets out of the account, unless the court immediately issues an order prohibiting you from transferring any assets, which ordinarily does not happen.

You can achieve a great measure of safety in an offshore bank account. You might have noticed that the banking crisis of the 1980s and 1990s is largely not an international one. Primarily, it is U.S. banks and savings and loans that are failing. Many foreign banks have established U.S. branches and invest in U.S. real estate. Yet these banks are not failing. That is because they operate under different rules and have more reasonable financial practices than even the strongest U.S. banks. In many developed countries, on the rare occasion

Using the Offshore Bank Account Loophole 29

when a bank fails, the major banks in the country take over its business to ensure that depositors do not lose any money. So if you are looking for banking safety, you should consider offshore banks.

An offshore bank can offer a measure of privacy that is not available in the United States. Many foreign countries ensure banking privacy in all but the most extreme situations. Austria, for example, allows bank accounts to be opened without a signature (although this may change within the next year or two). The person opening the account is given a number, and that number is all that is needed to make transactions. The account owner is the only one who knows the identity of the person behind the account. Some Hong Kong banks offer a similar kind of account, known as the "chop" account. A chop is a seal with a Chinese symbol or character on it. The bank honors all transaction orders that have the chop's imprint.

Switzerland recently changed its rules about numbered accounts. In the past, the fabled numbered Swiss account would be opened with only one bank officer knowing the true identity of the account owner. Those days are gone. Bank records now must record the identity of each account's owner. But numbered accounts still are available and provide a great deal of privacy.

OPENING THE OFFSHORE ACCOUNT

It is fairly simple to open an offshore bank account. Of course, you can go to the foreign country and visit the bank personally. This is the preferred method, as far as most bankers are concerned, and a number of foreign countries are now requiring that new customers appear in person to open accounts. The reason given is that bankers should know their customers so that they are not doing business with drug merchants, terrorists, and crooked politicians. You might also be able to open the account by mail, depending on the bank's rules. Most offshore banks will allow you to conduct transactions by mail, fax, or telex. But you might not be able to use these methods to open the account.

PRIVACY CONCERNS

The question that concerns many Americans is how to transfer their money to the account. You could, of course, simply write a check against your U.S. bank account or money market account. But if privacy is a reason for opening the account, writing a check against a not very private account defeats your purpose.

REPORTING CASH PAYMENTS

Under U.S. law, it is illegal to move $10,000 or more in cash (or cash equivalents) out of the country without filing the appropriate form—usually IRS Form 4789 or Customs Service Form 4790. The law also applies to traveler's checks, bearer bonds, and other securities negotiable either in the United States or abroad. U.S. banks making out a draft or a wire transfer on your behalf must also file the appropriate form. The maximum penalty for failure to do so is five years in jail and a fine of $500,000. It used to be that the simplest way legally to avoid creating an official record of your across-the-border transactions was to limit them to sizes of less than $10,000, but new legislation on money laundering prohibits structuring transactions to avoid the reporting. This law has stronger teeth than the reporting law itself, and a money-laundering conviction can result in a 20-year prison sentence and forfeiture of all of your property. And forget probation for first offenders. It not only doesn't exist any more, but federal judges are required to give the mandatory prison sentences specified in the laundering statute—the judge no longer has discretion in setting the sentence.

Remember, you can be guilty of laundering your own money—this isn't just a crime committed by a broker handling drug dealers' money for a fee. There have already been several convictions for money laundering of what would otherwise have been perfectly normal, legitimate transactions. One was the man who borrowed against his house, took the money in cash, and then made several separate cash deposits to his son's college account. Nothing wrong in the purpose, but the account was forfeited and he was convicted of a structured transaction to avoid reporting. Motive is irrelevant and was never even mentioned in the court case.

WIRE-TRANSFER WATCH

In 1990, at the orders of bank regulators, a new system of recording wire transfers was installed by U.S. banks. These movements of funds are normally used when speed is of the essence. Because banks themselves guarantee the fund's availability, wire transfers are accepted as cash. Of course, those asking their banks to wire money must pay a fee for the privilege.

Thanks to the new regulations, banks are now required to maintain extensive paperwork documenting the transfer. Of course, this means domestic wire-ransfer costs to the banks have gone up. The result is that many account holders have realized that these services will cost more. In effect, all users of wire transfers are being penalized so that the government, in its effort to crack down on drugs, can better record the movement of money between bank accounts.

INTERNATIONAL TRANSFERS

When regulations and procedures are in place (they are slowly being implemented), the same kind of surveillance will be introduced internationally. At present, only U.S. banks can be obliged by the authorities in this country to maintain such records. Foreign banks, regulated by their own authorities, are under no obligation to inform American bank examiners of the ownership of accounts they hold. The result is that increased information is available only on

Americans who send money overseas. Still, no one is able to determine to whom such transfers go or what they were for. Nor is anyone tracking wire transfers originating outside the United States—yet.

COVERING YOUR TRACKS

Your secret foreign bank account is not likely to remain a secret if you leave a string of canceled deposit checks from your U.S. bank. One way to avoid this is to deposit cash or an international money order. A U.S. Postal Service money order, for example, will do admirably. Just be sure to put an illegible scrawl in the space for the name of the buyer.

If someone you trust is willing to let you use his name, you can buy traveler's checks in his name and have him deposit them in your account. Another thing you can do is deposit in your overseas account an occasional check made out to you directly. This does leave a paper trail, but a rather unobtrusive one. The canceled check comes back to the issuing bank with the stamp of your overseas bank on it. It would take, however, an extraordinarily detailed audit of the person who wrote you the check—including reconciliation of all his bank statements—to uncover your connection to your offshore bank.

In some ways a simple personal check is better than it might seem at first. True, it leaves a trail on your account, but it is not automatically reported by anyone, with all the problems that creates. Or simply open a separate personal or business account to draw the checks sent abroad. And if you close the account after you are done with the transactions, and the account was in a distant state to start with, the account records go into the bank's dead file instead of the active computer, and eventually get destroyed. Money-market accounts with checking privileges also work extremely well for this purpose. You write a check from your personal account to the money-market fund, use one of its checks to send the money abroad, and then close the money-market account. This is clearly legal and avoids any issue of what is or is not structuring with money orders. The paper trail does exist, but it takes a massive amount of work to follow it.

REPORTING FOREIGN BANK ACCOUNTS

Another law, the already discussed U.S. Banking Secrecy Act, covers foreign bank accounts. It requires Americans to report ownership of non-U.S. bank accounts valued at $10,000 or more. You have no reporting requirement as long as the per person total in all foreign bank accounts does not exceed $10,000 at any point in a tax year. That means every member of a family can have his or her own foreign account. This threshold applies to the sum of all accounts plus certificates of deposit (CDs). It also includes the cash and negotiable securities in securities accounts. The penalties for not complying are the same as those for illegally exporting funds but not as severe as the new money-laundering penalties.

Here also, the simplest way to avoid the reporting requirement legally is to make sure that your balance remains below $10,000. However, that may be more difficult than it seems: uncertainties arise in calculating the exchange rate you must use in converting the deutsche marks or the yen in your account.

Unfortunately, you cannot use the exchange rate printed in the financial section of the newspaper. You must use the official rates calculated by the Federal Reserve Bank of New York. The problem is that those rates are not released until well after the year is over. By the time you find out what exchange rate the government will use to value your account, it is too late to make any downward adjustments in your balance.

The only solution to this problem is to leave yourself a conservative margin by staying well below the reporting threshold. If your account approaches the limit, transfer some money to your spouse or your children. If a foreign currency appreciates against the dollar and you earn interest besides, you may have to reduce your overseas holdings to stay under the ceiling.

INVESTING TO STAY UNDER THE MINIMUM

Another thing you can do is invest some of your balance. The $10,000 ceiling does not apply to foreign stocks, bonds, mutual funds, and investment funds that you may own—as long as they are not in a foreign securities account or a foreign bank account. A securities account includes a brokerage account, but also things like a foreign bank acting as securities custodian. It would not be inconceivable that a foreign accountant or lawyer holding securities as your nominee could be deemed to be a securities account, and you probably don't want to be the first test case.

If you are in danger of hitting the ceiling, buy a bond or a mutual fund and take delivery of the certificate. It can be sent by registered mail to your address in the United States. Or it can be sent to an officer of an overseas bank, who will accept it on your behalf and hold it until you can pick it up at some future date. As long as it needs your physical endorsement to be negotiated, that temporary holding is probably not a securities account.

Put the bond or stock certificate in a safe-deposit box, and then it won't be in a securities account. This strategy will not work with most foreign mutual funds because most of them do not issue certificates, but a direct fund holding registered in your name is a shareholding, not a securities account.

In addition, many countries, including France, have eliminated the issue of stock and bond certificates entirely. You cannot take delivery because the securities exist only in book-entry form. A great number of countries in Europe are moving toward paperless securities in book-entry form. This distinction between securities inside and outside an account results from the U.S. government's mistaken premise that any negotiable instrument in a securities account is as liquid as cash.

EXPATRIATE VIOLATION

In practice, Americans living overseas are the most frequent violators of the reporting requirement. Thousands of them exceed the $10,000 threshold at some time or another. Moreover, overseas IRS offices do not routinely inform Americans about the reporting rules. Also, the U.S. Treasury is not particularly interested in trying to track down every expatriate whose bank balance exceeds the ceiling from time to time and who fails to report.

The U.S. Treasury, in its own words, is looking for "systematic, deliberate violations of the law." To date, the most the Treasury has been able to recover through lawsuits against violators was the amount of their unreported foreign balances. There never has been a prosecution of an expatriate lacking significant U.S. assets—probably because the Treasury is uncertain whether it would be able to collect abroad, even if a U.S. court were to rule in its favor. There may, however, have been out-of-court settlements. But with the new emphasis on this area, you might find your passport revoked or not renewed, forcing you back to the United States to stand trial.

TAX CONCERNS

As a U.S. citizen, you are taxed by the United States on your worldwide income. This includes interest and other income earned by the offshore bank account. That's not a big problem, and you probably are prepared for it. Don't fall for the argument some promoters make that you can open the account, let interest accumulate for a few years, and then spend the income tax-free overseas. If the IRS finds out about this, it can prosecute you for tax fraud.

The interest earned on the foreign account probably will

be paid or credited to you in a foreign currency. For tax purposes, you have to value it in U.S. dollars, using one of two exchange rates. If you bring the money back to the United States, you use the rate that prevails at the time of the transfer. If you do not bring the money back, you use the official exchange rate calculated by the New York Federal Reserve.

Avoiding Double Taxation

Be aware that the foreign government with jurisdiction over your non-U.S. bank may impose its own withholding taxes. Switzerland, for example, withholds 35 percent of your interest earnings at the source. If the country in question has a double-taxation treaty with the United States, you may qualify for a deduction on your U.S. return, but then you also have to declare the existence of your bank account.

(The amount you can recover varies from country to country according to the terms of whatever treaty is in force at the time. However, you are unlikely to recover more than a fraction of what was withheld in the first place.)

SELECTING A BANK

The bank you choose depends upon your goals. If you want maximum privacy and protection from the U.S. government, the courts, and anyone who might win a court judgment against you, you do not want to use an offshore bank that has branches or subsidiaries in the United States. The U.S. courts have been known to threaten the demise of U.S. branches or subsidiaries if the offshore parent company does not comply with U.S. orders. But if you want an easy and fast way to set up an offshore account, you want to use a foreign bank that has U.S. branches, or you might want to use a major U.S. bank that has foreign offices or subsidiaries. This allows you to walk into a U.S. office and have that office assist you in setting up the offshore account.

You probably also want to check the fees at several banks before selecting one. In a number of countries, banking fees can be rather expensive, far more expensive than what many Americans are used to paying. Any investment and tax advantages of the offshore account might be seriously diminished by high fees.

GETTING YOUR MONEY OUT

If you are using your haven account only to trade international stocks, getting your money out of this account is no different than making a withdrawal from your local bank. You merely request a check in the currency of your choice and deposit it wherever you like.

If financial privacy is your concern, you don't want a haven-account check with your name on it floating around the U.S. or Canadian banking system. It leaves an audit trail that will reveal your secret.

The easiest way to avoid such a trail is to restrict yourself to cash withdrawals in person. A more convenient course would be to inquire whether your haven bank can issue you a VISA or American Express card. When the bill for your charges on such a card is presented to your bank, it is paid out of your account.

You can spend your haven money in this way, wherever such cards are honored. Moreover, these transactions clear offshore—beyond the scrutiny of North American officials.

THE ULTIMATE OFFSHORE BANK LOOPHOLE

Suppose you don't want to simply open a foreign bank account. Suppose you want to bank offshore, but you want some more control of your money. One option a number of Americans have proposed is ownership of an offshore bank.

Owning a bank is a lot easier in many countries than it is in the United States. Some countries cater to individual foreigners who want to own banks, streamlining chartering rules and making the cost an affordable $20,000 or so.

Many people who have opened their own offshore

banks have improperly used the banks to defraud others or to evade their taxes. Banking havens take precautions to ensure that you do not conduct any banking business with their citizens. But that doesn't mean you have to use the bank improperly. It can be a real bank with a genuine charter, capable of joining the world of international banking. It can take deposits, make loans, issue letters of credit, and invest money.

Here's the best part for U.S. citizens: offshore banking income is not presently considered subpart F income. In the chapter on the United States as a tax haven, we discuss how when an offshore corporation is controlled by U.S. citizens, the subpart F income passes through to the U.S. shareholders as though it were a partnership. But banking income is not subpart F income. The profits accumulate in the offshore bank and are compounded free of U.S. taxes. If you set up the bank in the right country, your taxes will be low in your home country. Careful investing and use of tax treaties should eliminate or reduce taxes from other countries.

But to qualify for the exception from subpart F, your bank must conduct real business. This means that you have to solicit business from independent parties. You have to get deposits and make loans. If the parties involved are not independent of the bank's owners, the IRS likely will say that it is simply an offshore investment corporation and not a bank and will tax U.S. shareholders on the corporation's income.

To start a foreign bank properly, you need at least $250,000 in start-up capital. You also need professional advice to select the right country for incorporation and to find someone to manage the bank in that country. One of the real advantages of an offshore bank is that you do not need a walk-in retail operation, such as that of your neighborhood bank. Most offshore banking transactions are done through modern electronic communications. The occasional client who wants to visit the bank will be satisfied with an office that looks like any other professional office.

Using the Offshore Bank Account Loophole 39

Because of its attacks on drug dealers and their financial operations, the United States is constantly lobbying countries with liberal banking rules to change them. Therefore, many of the Caribbean countries that used to be ideal for setting up private offshore banks are now fairly inconvenient to use. They require more start-up capital than they used to, and they might not even want to give you a charter. But if you are serious about operating an offshore bank and if you seek help from someone who is up on the international banking situation, you might find that the private offshore bank is the ultimate offshore loophole.

If you don't think of major industrialized countries as secrecy havens, you are overlooking a valuable strategy. Rather than doing your banking in an attention-attracting haven like the Bahamas or the Cayman Islands, there is much to be said for quietly opening a normal account in almost any country outside the United States. Almost all respect privacy more than the United States does, and your dealings with the bank will not be particularly noteworthy. Every country has lots of American residents who open bank accounts for one reason or another. If you create your own privacy haven in this way instead of joining the crowd writing to the latest bank to be touted in a privacy newsletter, you will be much better off. Very few countries (with the exception of Switzerland) tax the bank accounts of nonresidents. Even the United States does not tax foreigner's bank accounts in this country. Choose a country because of family or business ties, and you have another reason for the particular account that helps it to blend in. On this basis, lots of places are practical: Germany, France, Belgium, the Netherlands, Argentina, Mexico, Australia, Singapore . . . you get the idea.

CHAPTER 5
NAIVE FOOLS SPEND TIME IN PRISON

One of the greatest problems of offshore privacy strategic planning is the naive fool who breaks laws without thinking through the consequences. For example, as a consultant, I once had a call from a certified public accountant in a major U.S. city who said he had a number of clients who wanted to establish "secret" bank accounts in the Cayman Islands. He said his clients were paying all their taxes but were very concerned with secrecy and wanted to be certain that the U.S. government would not learn about the accounts.

He became greatly offended when I explained to him that all his clients were crooks. I explained in detail that no U.S. citizen (or resident) could have a "secret" bank account because it is a felony to fail to notify the government immediately of the existence of the account. The penalties for such secrecy at that time were far worse than any possible tax offense—today the penalties have been increased so severely that no American should even contemplate such a violation. One bribed bank clerk (perhaps for a mere $100) in a so-called secrecy jurisdiction could put the client in prison for 10 to 15 years under new mandatory minimum sentencing laws. There are numerous legitimate ways that a U.S. citizen can make foreign investments without running afoul of these draconian laws, many of which are discussed in *The Tax Haven Report* and *The Tax Exile Report*. (Both of these books are published by Scope International Ltd., 62 Murray Road, Waterlooville, Hants PO8 9JL, Great Britain. The company will send you a free copy of these and similar titles.)

The most dangerous fools—to themselves as well as to everyone they deal with—are those individuals who fail to understand the serious implications of their actions. They deal with lawyers, accountants, and/or bankers as if there was nothing legally wrong with their actions and then seem startled when the family accountant or banker facing many years in prison testifies against them because he was dragged into something he had no intention of being a part of. Or worse, they wind up blurting out their incriminating intentions to a lawyer or accountant who immediately notifies the authorities, frequently setting a trap for them. (Remember, lawyer-client confidentiality does not apply to stating an intention to commit a crime, and the lawyer is legally obligated to report it.) Many U.S. professionals today (perhaps fearing a possible setup by authorities) err on the side of caution and immediately report such approaches. This is no secret—it has been recorded in many, many court cases—but naive clients continue to get convicted.

The penalties for most of the bank secrecy and money-laundering crimes (money laundering includes moving unreported cash, even if you are the legal owner) are several times the penalty for armed bank robbery.

Most of these people would never consider committing a bank robbery, and if they were to plan such a crime, they would choose their partners with extreme care and full awareness of the consequences by all parties concerned. Yet they think nothing of committing financial crimes with far more serious penalties, and cavalierly involving others, as if it was a big joke and nothing to be seriously concerned about.

There are enough legal means to accomplish the same ends that nobody needs to commit these crimes. But if they persist in doing so, they should at least face the reality of their acts and plan like real criminals, choosing their associates with the same care they would use to choose bank robbery partners. If you really want to be a criminal, then be one, but don't stagger around the offshore banking world like a drunken water buffalo.

If you want to gain a good understanding of how the government views tax havens, University Microfilms International, through its Books on Demand program, is now making available *Tax Havens and Their Uses by United States Taxpayers* by Richard Gordon. Frequently referred to as "The Gordon Report," the U.S. Treasury Department prepared this 1981 study at the request of Congress. It gives considerable detail and examples of the uses of tax havens. Anyone interested in tax havens who has not studied this work will find much still useful information in it. Although it has been out of print for more than a decade, copies can be ordered through booksellers or directly from University Microfilms International, 300 North Zeeb Road, Ann Arbor, Michigan 48106-1346; (800) 521-0600 or (313) 761-4700. The UMI catalog number of the book is AU00435, and UMI accepts Visa or MasterCard.

CHAPTER 6
PRUDENT WAYS FOR AMERICANS TO BUY OFFSHORE FUNDS

Eventually one needs to make a direct foreign investment. Buying United States-based global or international mutual funds is a useful currency diversification and a helpful way for the smaller investor to get started. But since these funds are still a U.S. asset, such fund investments do not help to diversify your assets in an asset-protection sense, safeguarding against lawsuits, forfeitures, possible future exchange controls, or any other contingencies.

It is not illegal for Americans to buy offshore mutual funds (called unit trusts in some countries) or any other security that is not registered for sale in the United States. Most foreign securities that are not mutual funds can be bought through any good stockbroker, although you can do better if you select a broker who specializes in foreign securities. But he can't sell you a foreign mutual fund. That doesn't mean that there is something dirty or illegal about it; it merely means that the fund is not registered for sale in the United States.

There are a number of reasons for this. Expense is one; successful foreign funds don't need the U.S. market and see little reason to pay the outrageous fees of our litigious society. (Some of the best foreign cars cannot be purchased in the U.S. for a similar reason. The makers of $100,000 custom cars are not about to give the federal government 10 free cars

45

per year for destruction testing.) Some of the funds cannot meet U.S. legal requirements because they charge investors a performance fee rather than a management fee based on a percentage of assets. But many investors would actually prefer a fund manager whose only compensation is a share of the profits instead of a fee based on the total investments in the fund. The manager's goals are different.

It is illegal for a foreign securities issuer, such as a mutual fund, to sell an unregistered security in the United States. To be completely safe, most (but not all) of them refuse to sell to an American citizen or resident even if he is residing abroad. They'd rather stay away from anything to do with Americans. To protect themselves, they require a statement on the application that the purchaser is not a resident or citizen of the United States.

Some advisors suggest using a mail-forwarding service in a foreign country, and simply signing a false declaration. It is probably quite safe to do so, but such dishonesty could turn out to be imprudent later. To take an extreme example (at least we hope it is an extreme example), some other country could suddenly adopt American-style forfeiture laws and decide that securities procured by fraud were forfeitable to the government. (The false declaration is clearly a fraudulent statement, even if there is no financial loss to the seller.)

This example might seem extreme, but a recent U.S. case presents a scary analogy. A mortgage applicant in 1986 made an allegedly false statement about his employment. In 1992, the federal government confiscated the house on the grounds that the false employment statement was fraud on a federally insured bank, even though the mortgage had been paid. The householder claimed that he had worked for the company off the books, but the payroll records did not support his claim. The U.S. Court of Appeals ruled in 1993 that the house was subject to administrative forfeiture by the government and that the owner was not entitled to a hearing or trial or to present his defense to a court.

Looked at in another way, although the purchase of the securities by an American is not illegal, it would not be impossible for the U.S. government to argue that the securities are subject to forfeiture on the grounds that the purchaser committed mail fraud by mailing a false declaration of citizenship. The U.S. Supreme Court has long ruled that mail fraud need not involve a monetary loss, but only the mailing of a false statement with an intangible gain (in this example, the ownership of a security that could not have been obtained without the false statement). Thus all the legal elements of proof for a mail-fraud case would have been met. More likely than a mail-fraud prosecution, however, would be a civil forfeiture of the security, similar to the mortgage example above. And why contaminate an honest investment by taking even the slightest risk of acquiring it in an illegal manner? There is no reason to do so, when the entire transaction can be conducted honestly, legally, and properly.

These horror stories may seem far-fetched examples, but the house-seizure case would suggest that they may not be.

So how can an American purchase these securities legally? There are two possible routes that meet the legal requirements.

The first is to use a foreign bank or trust company as a nominee holder. In this example the nominee holds the security under a simple agreement for the true owner. This is technically a form of trust but is normally limited to a one- or two-paragraph standard agreement form used by the bank. This strategy would not be valid if the form required by the offshore fund included a statement that the beneficial owner is not an American. Most of these fund statements do not go that far, but some of them do (in particular the Fidelity group offshore-based funds) because they are part of a U.S. parent company.

The second strategy is a more sophisticated version of the first. A simple trust is created, with the foreign bank or trust company acting as trustee and the beneficiary being the U.S. holder, with a spouse and/or children being contingent beneficiaries in case of death. Now the trust itself is the legal and the beneficial owner, and the requirements of the fund have been met. The fact that the trust has American beneficiaries is not legally the same as the shares being beneficially owned by an American.

Such agreements are usually simple, and most major foreign banks can deal with them. For example, banks in Canada,

Britain, and Hong Kong will usually charge only around $500 to set up a trust, and around $50 or $100 per year per security for nominee agreements. A Swiss bank could also act as a nominee.

Canada and Britain have been mentioned in the example for a reason. It is not necessary to go to a tax haven for this kind of service. Very few countries are interested in taxing a trust in which the assets and the beneficiaries are foreign, so even a high-tax country will usually qualify for this type of simple trust or nominee arrangement. The bank will be able to tell you the local tax position for such an arrangement.

The banks in the high-tax countries tend to be far cheaper—this is as routine as asking your local bank's trust department to hold a share certificate for your children—and you avoid the high trust formation fees that most tax havens charge.

In theory a Swiss bank could be a trustee rather than a nominee, but this gets into some exotic legal questions of civil-versus-common-law countries because the IRS will only recognize a common-law trust.

By using either of the approaches outlined and staying in a common-law country (Britain and the countries that inherited the British legal system, e.g., the United States), the trust is neutral or transparent for tax purposes. The value of this is that you can then claim a U.S. tax credit for any foreign withholding taxes paid by the trust, although normally the point of offshore funds is that there are no withholding taxes.

One of the best ways to purchase offshore mutual funds or make any offshore investment is a Swiss product just announced. Jurg Lattmann, founder of JML Swiss Investment Counsellors (Dept. 212, Germaniastrase 55, 8033 Zurich, Switzerland), has teamed up with the Swiss bank Ueberseebank to create BankSwiss, an account designed specifically for foreign investors.

BankSwiss is a special Swiss bank account that pays no Swiss withholding tax, is completely private and liquid at all times, can be switched between all of the major currencies, and keeps your capital fully invested at all times. It hass a low minimum of U.S $10,000, which entitles you to an international credit card good for purchases or withdrawals from your local ATM.

CHAPTER 7
GREAT BRITAIN

The principles of British banking secrecy are summed up in a famous legal case that began in April 1922 with a dishonored check for £9, 8 shillings, 6 pence. The poor man, whose name was Tournier, signed an agreement with the bank in which he undertook to pay back £1 a week, starting from when he began a new job, for a period of three months. He was also to give the bank the name and address of his new employer.

Unfortunately, he failed to make one of his repayments, and the manager of the bank telephoned his employer to advise him of this situation. During the course of the conversation, the banker also implied that Tournier had issued some substantial checks to bookmakers. Because of these comments, Tournier's employer declined to renew his contract of employment when it expired. Tournier sued the bank. During the judicial proceedings that followed, the banker and two directors of the employer's company all admitted the substance of the conversation, and the directors further confirmed that this was the reason for the nonrenewal of Tournier's contract.

The court dismissed Tournier's action at the first hearing. On appeal, however, the court ruled in his favor. This decision set out the principles of British banking secrecy. Not only did Tournier finally obtain justice, but he won a place in British history on the strength of a check of less than £10—which is a fairly cheap cost for immortality.

The Tournier decision also set forth four instances in which the banker is "relieved" of banking secrecy: 1) by order of the law, 2) through duty to the public, 3) in the interests of the bank, and 4) if the client's express or implicit permission has been given. British tax inspectors do not have a general right of examination and cannot seek more than the identities of the true owners. If the inspector of taxes sees that the account holder is not a British resident, he immediately stops his inquiries and files his papers, in spite of all the splendid double tax agreements signed by Britain under which information is supposed to be exchanged.

If you are interested in a foreign bank account protected from U.S. withholding taxes and covered by laws protecting privacy, you can easily open one in Britain (and not have to worry about a foreign language). Unfortunately, the situation in Britain is among the most subject to change under pressure from the United States.

THE NEW BRITISH REGULATIONS

Britain's banking supervision is handled by the Bank of England, which operates under a suspicion-based system. That means that a tip-off from the police or other authorities is the usual way that the banks find out that money deposited with them has been illicitly gained. (The United States and Canada require reporting of all deposits above a certain size.)

British banks are in line with current global measures to reduce money laundering. In 1989, an official banking circular (which is nothing to sneeze at in Britain) was sent by the Bank of England to British banks. It pointed out that the provisions of the Basle Statement of January 1989 endorsed by the governors of the central banks, including that of Britain, provided that banks must report suspicions when they have reason to believe that funds derived from criminal activities are being deposited with them.

The Bank of England circular stressed that a statutory exemption from suits by clients angered at the lifting of banking confidentiality already exists under law in such cases. The circular also called for banks to train their personnel about bank policy in this area. (Most of the time, the lowest-level bank tellers receive the large cash deposits of a potentially suspect nature.)

Despite the circular, British parliamentarians are anxious to have more done. The House of Commons Home Affairs Select Committee urged that the Bank of England conduct an investigation of money laundering. The Parliamentarians are worried about destabilization of small British banks if money is impounded.

THE NORIEGA CONNECTION

Adding fuel to the fire was the decision not to crack down immediately in Britain on the Bank of Credit and Commerce International (BCCI), which had 42 branches in Britain. BCCI was headquartered through a Luxembourg holding company. Two of its subsidiaries, in the United States and Grand Cayman, have pleaded guilty in U.S. courts to deliberate money laundering on behalf of Gen. Manuel Noriega and the Medellín drug cartel.

USING A BRITISH BANK TO CIRCUMVENT FRENCH EXCHANGE CONTROLS

At a party in Paris, an African man asked a friend if she had a Swiss bank account. Naturally, she said no. He then explained that he needed to transfer money to his aged mother in Lagos, Nigeria. Because he lived and worked in France, the exchange controls prevented him from getting his money out.

At that time, French banks would allow you to transfer funds out of the country, but only less than a certain low amount. Although you could request an exemption on humanitarian grounds, the procedure was complicated, costly, and time consuming. After enduring these headaches, there was no guarantee that your request would be granted. Our African acquaintance could not legally send a check to his mother because French customs was scanning the mail at the border.

As it turned out, there was no need to have a Swiss bank account to make the transfer. Our friend was able to arrange it by writing a letter to her London bank. The Nigerian paid her the money she laid out on his behalf as well as the bank charges incurred, and his mother received a draft on a bank in Lagos.

PRIVATE BANKING IN WOOD-PANELED SPLENDOR

This same friend opened her first foreign bank account in Britain at Child & Company (subsequently bought by William's and then by Glynn's, Mills and then amalgamated with the Royal Bank of Scotland) shortly after she married an Englishman. Her parents, worried that she would not be able to return home if she changed her mind, gave her a check for the airfare as a backhanded wedding gift.

Her husband, who already had an account there, accompanied her to the bank. At the door they were greeted by an elderly doorman in a uniform that would have done honor to a Guardsman at Buckingham Palace. He regaled them with his memories of her husband's grandfather, the General, and led them to the manager's office.

In his mahogany-wainscoted office, surrounded by scratchy horsehair sofas, polished brass, stained glass, and yellowed ledgers into which Dickensian clerks were writing with quill pens, her husband was mellow and affable. He made sure that her money was in her name. All of this spectacle and service were due to a total deposit that was the sum for a single one-way airfare.

The point is this: Without some sort of introduction or at least a letter from your bank manager at home, you will not

Great Britain

be able to open an account with Child or Rothschilds or Coutts or William's & Glynn's. You probably will not be much better off in the provinces either, with the likes of Edinburgh's licensed deposit-taker Adam & Company, for instance.

In fact, the smaller British private banks are the most difficult for an outsider to deal with because they cannot cope with a lot of customers. As a result, they screen customers with particular care. It helps to have dealings with U.S. banks that are part of the private bank network, such as Brown Brothers, Harriman & Co. (as opposed to the big banks that are aggressively seeking private accounts from high-net-worth individuals, but lack correspondent relations with the smaller British, Swiss, Austrian, and German banks).

Small British banks usually do not have facilities offshore in places such as the Channel Islands or the Isle of Man (the subject of a separate chapter). If they do, they carefully hive them off from the wood-paneled discretion of headquarters.

In fact, British small bankers may not be the best people to go to for transactions involving foreign exchange—the very transactions that you as a foreigner are most likely to need. The Royal Bank of Scotland may offer high-yield money-market checking accounts in Jersey (that is old Jersey, a Channel Island, not New Jersey), but Messrs. Child are offering a wholly different service to a different clientele.

The British private banks controlled by the large clearing banks (Barclays, Lloyds, National Westminster, Standard Chartered, and the two Scottish banks, Bank of Scotland and Royal Bank of Scotland) tend to be much more profitable than their parents. That is one reason why other entities such as Kleinwort Benson, a "merchant bank" (meaning an investment bank in U.S. usage) form their own private banking units.

National Westminster operates Coutts & Company, which has celebrated its 300th birthday, and includes the royal family among its clients. There is nothing quite so chic as banking with Coutts, but you will have to be introduced.

Lloyds and Barclays also have separate private banking divisions. Standard does not have a separate private banking office. Child & Company, which was established during the fifteenth century, is now a subsidiary of the Royal Bank of Scotland. It has offices at Oxford to attract the collegians who will go on to earn great wealth, and its main headquarters is at 1 Fleet Street in London.

Only Hoare & Company, established in 1672, is a family-owned banking partnership, which some people think is the only kind of private bank to deal with. Contact managing partner Henry C. Hoare if you think you qualify for his attention. The Royal Family maintain accounts with Mr. Hoare.

CATERING A WAKE

It is rumored that, for the right client, British private banks will arrange everything from negotiating marriage settlements to hiring a nanny, from ensuring boarding school admission to catering a wake. For a fee, they will do property management and portfolio operations.

One of the myths surrounding international banking is that you have to go to Switzerland to get privacy and service. It is true that British courts may lift bank secrecy for a foreign subpoena—but then again they may not.

The U.S. Treasury maintains a large staff in Grosvenor Square (the U.S. Embassy in London) precisely because British cooperation with U.S. authorities is not automatic. For normal amounts owned by law-abiding Americans, Britain offers a high degree of privacy. When people have broken the law, it is up to the U.S. authorities to prove to a British judge that a violation has occurred. They cannot just demand data on U.S. account holders. Nor can they just go rummaging about on what is popularly called a "fishing expedition" in hope of uncovering some wrongdoing.

NO WITHHOLDING TAXES

British bankers—even onshore—will not ask for your Social Security number. Nor will they charge withholding tax

Great Britain 55

on interest they pay on your nonresident account. This makes them far better for most customers than Swiss banks—which subject foreigners to a 35-percent withholding. (For British residents, the banks now pay interest without deducting the withholding tax because not every resident is liable for taxation.)

Just specify when you open your account (checking or savings) that you are a nonresident and show your passport. Britain, like the United States, does not require people to have identity cards and registration to show where they live. A passport will be accepted as adequate. (On the Continent, proving that you are a nonresident—or even becoming one—can be more complicated. It takes two years after you have left France to become a nonresident if you have lived there.)

You may get the highest yields from the British equivalents of savings and loans, called building societies (which now offer limited checking), and from banks that specialize in high-yield banking by mail. The pioneer in this business is another Scottish bank, the Bank of Scotland (which is a normal bank despite the official-sounding name).

INVESTMENT SERVICES

The Bank of Scotland offers an excellent means of buying good British mutual funds. They operate something called "Number One Savings Scheme" with Ivory & Sime, an investment trust group (investment trusts are quoted closed-ended mutual funds). This program allows you to invest £250 or more or £20 per month or more in funds run by Ivory & Sime and to reinvest the dividends.

Purchases of funds are at a lower commission rate than if you went on your own to a broker because small orders are consolidated once a month. You can take the dividends of one fund and invest them in another, subject to a minimum of £20. Different Ivory & Sime investment trusts focus on U.S. shares, British shares, European shares, smaller European companies, unlisted European stocks, high-yield stocks, and energy stocks.

There also is a fund aimed at private investors, the Personal Assets Trust. There are no money-market funds because the bank prefers for you to keep the money on deposit. For high yields, you can maintain deposits in any currency you want. Other large British banks (called clearing banks) may soon get into investment services to compete.

British banks will hold stocks and bonds and mutual funds ("unit trusts" in Britain if they are open ended) that their foreign clients have purchased and will collect dividends and interest. Interest on bank accounts is paid to nonresidents without deductions for taxes. Dividends on British shares are paid without withholding tax. To get reimbursed for the British tax credit (a further 40 percent in dividend), you have to file for relief from the British Inland Revenue Service, which will inform the authorities of your country of tax payment. (The tax credit is payable to shareholders to reimburse them for the corporate taxes already paid by the company in which they own stock. Shareholders in the United States get no such relief.)

COMMUNICATING WITH SHAREHOLDERS

British banks are also better than continentals at keeping in touch with shareholders on behalf of companies. In Britain, as in the United States, nominative rolls of company shareholders are kept, if not by the corporation, at least by its nominees.

(On the Continent, bearer shares are more usual, which means that you don't get proxy statements, annual or quarterly reports, or any information about shareholders' ordinary or extraordinary meetings. Also, no one can get in touch with you to mount a takeover bid on your company.)

If a British bank holds non-British shares for you—even ones traded in London—the situation is more complicated. Dividends are payable in a foreign currency and

Great Britain 57

subject to withholding tax under the dual taxation rate applying between Britain and the third country. That makes it better, for example, to hold most non-ADR Spanish stocks through Britain. In some cases, it is better to hold shares in the United States than in England. In other cases, the dual taxation treaty favors holding the stock in the United Kingdom. Ask which is best before deciding where to domicile your investment. Your nice British bank will charge you the fee levied by its local agents in the third country, plus an exchange commission and a collection commission.

It will not charge you a high commission for converting the foreign dividend into sterling—as a U.S. bank would do even for a dividend in Canadian dollars. Foreign exchange conversion fees are considerably lower than those applying in most other countries as well, possibly including Switzerland. They still may dissuade you from owning a diversified international portfolio out of London or anywhere else.

BRITISH MUTUAL FUNDS

One way around this is to consider a mutual fund. British onshore portfolio managers and British stockbrokers (for stocks or investment trusts) are happy to open accounts for you. A British brokerage house, Olliff & Partners, specializes in research into British closed-end funds ("investment trusts" in the local version of English). Because the British (in fact, the Scots) invented mutual funds, there are far more investment trusts trading in London than there are closed-end funds trading in New York, 217 at last count. A number of them specialize in investment in foreign (i.e., non-British) markets. This is a painless way into European equities for Americans.

Olliff practices asset-based research to try to seek out funds that are particularly good values (i.e., penalized unfairly by a discount in the market). They also seek funds liable to be liquidated, turned into split capital funds, open-ended, or bought for their assets by other funds, companies (sometimes ones in which the fund is heavily invested), or even brokerage houses. Under British law a brokerage firm such as Olliff can (and does) mount takeover bids on investment trusts.

Unlike American closed-end funds, investment trusts can borrow to invest to enhance their returns. Capital gains tax is not payable by trusts on gains realized within the portfolio. Most of the dividends received are distributed to the trusts' shareholders. Management charges are low compared to those of open-ended funds ("unit trusts"). Dealing costs are the same as for any other entity.

Olliff & Partners also does standard stock market trading in nonfund shares. Unlike many post-Big Bang brokers, Olliff is looking for retail clients. We think the main specialty it offers should be carefully considered as a vehicle for creating a diversified international portfolio. Contact Lorraine Goodhew, Olliff & Partners, Saddlers House, Gutter Lane, Cheapside, London EC2V 6BR, England; tel. (44-71) 374-0191; fax (44-71) 374-2063.

You will have to go through a brokerage house or bank to make your initial purchase in a British investment trust. Like a U.S. closed-end fund, it is publicly traded on the stock exchange and may frequently trade at a discount to net-asset value. Of course, when you sell or switch between funds, you may face an even bigger discount. In the interval, you will have more money working for you than you are investing.

FAMILIARITY WITH FOREIGNERS

Investment trust managers don't normally panic at a request for information from the United States. These firms are used to dealing with masses of small investors, and one more seems to be no particular problem. Furthermore, the fact that they are onshore and regulated seems to mean less surveillance from the British authorities and less suspicion from the U.S. Securities Exchange Commission (SEC). (The same is not true of all unit trusts, the equivalent of open-ended mutual funds, which are sold directly and are not quoted on the stock exchange.)

Investment trusts are not all created equal. It may be hard to get your money out of some of the smaller trusts, which require written withdrawal and may have a notice period. Furthermore, British investment trusts may be more than 100-percent invested. That is, they may borrow money to buy additional shares. That increases the leverage and the risk.

ENGLISH SPOKEN HERE

Another advantage of banking in Britain is that prospectuses are in English. Moreover, the accounts of the investment trusts are subject to the Securities and Investment Board (SIB), the newly created British equivalent of the SEC, which means that they are audited and registered annually, if not more often. However, they are not registered with the SEC. It may reassure you to know that the auditors of the investment trusts listed below are international firms like Arthur Young & Co.

Many investment trusts are located not in London, but around Charlotte Square in Edinburgh, Scotland. One reason may be to be closer to the shade of Adam Smith. Another may be that good stock market thinking is easier to do away from the pressure of constant trading. (We see the same phenomenon in the Netherlands, where the biggest fund is run out of Rotterdam, not the financial capital.)

We already mentioned Ivory & Sime, established in 1898 (which invented the first fund for non-Japanese investing in Japan), of 1 Charlotte Square, Edinburgh, Scotland; tel. (44-31) 225-1357; fax (44-3) 225-2375. It now has a group of 12 investment trusts, and you can switch among them without fees. Another Scottish group is Dunedin (which runs five trusts, among them The Edinburgh Investment Trust, second largest in the United Kingdom), 25 Ravelson Terrace; tel. (44-31) 315-2500; fax (44-31) 315-2222. Both of the canny Scottish groups welcome U.S. investors and boast that they have many. They also manage money for U.S. insurance companies. British Linen Bank, a subsidiary of the Bank of Scotland, has now acquired 50.5 percent of the Dunedin group. The British Linen Bank has opened a series of U.S. branches.

These Scottish groups produce daily calculations of net-asset value. That means that it is very easy to figure whether your shares are trading at a discount or a premium. This is in sharp contrast to some other investment trusts, which, according to a recent study by Nigel Russell of James Capel (a London brokerage house), tally up the worth of their portfolios only once a month.

For investment trusts, small is not necessarily beautiful. Good managers want to know where they stand and to let their shareholders know, too. The *Financial Times* of London publishes weekly net-asset value figures.

BORROWING FROM BRITISH BANKS

Another convenience of a British bank account is a VISA or American Express card or a MasterCard in either dollars or sterling drawn on your British bank account. Britain's Access system (as its name implies) gives you access to a gold MasterCard—and also to the network Eurocard in other European countries.

You have to pay your bill by check or bank transfer, as you do for American Express in the United States. You cannot have your bank account debited directly as you can with a card granted by a bank where you have an account (in the United States or on the Continent). On one hand, this gives you greater control of the debits. On the other, you are more likely to incur interest charges because of the way the mail behaves.

Just having a foreign currency credit card offers a lot of

advantages. You can bring your money home without using the banking system to do so (and leaving records that may interest the tax man) by the simple device of spending it—or using a cash machine that accepts your British card and British PIN code (in the United States or elsewhere).

British banks love to lend you money and will do so if you overdraw. Overdraft loans are available from any British bank that has confidence in you as a customer. (It is a good idea to talk about your plans to overdraw in advance—but the whole idea will be reasonably well received in Britain.)

Of course, banks will charge you a hefty rate of interest for your overdraft. The total amount of the loan will be exactly the amount needed to balance your account—not the next round number as with U.S. credit cards. Furthermore, there are no little bank charges of $25 for going into the red and $20 or so for every bounced check, as there are with our homegrown bankers. For more information on acquiring an overseas credit card (VISA), contact Lloyds Bank, 39 Threadneedle Street, London EC2R 8AU; tel. (44-71) 628-7755; fax (44-71) 588-8218; M.G. Hardman, manager.

HOME MORTGAGES

British banks can lend you money to buy houses in or outside Britain. Coutts & Company, a firm of private bankers specializing in customers worth £30,000 per year or more (about $50,000), boasts that it will arrange a mortgage of £250,000 ($400,000) in a little over two hours. British building societies will also offer you mortgage financing for buying property in Britain or even outside Britain.

One result of British deregulation is that a lot of new players have entered the mortgage business and often are willing to cut rates to win customers. A lot of money is available from insurance companies, directly or in conjunction with banks. Much of this business is run from British offshore islands. Another entrant in this market is the British subsidiary of Chemical Bank of New York, which is proud of offering great flexibility in arranging mortgage finance for expatriates.

To save on taxes and interest, it is often best to borrow in the United States against an existing property by taking a home-equity loan to buy a foreign property. Under the tax reform law, your interest payments to a British bank for a mortgage on a principal or a secondary residence should be tax deductible in the United States. (Most British mortgages are at floating rates and in sterling. You must calculate an interest with an exchange risk if you are paying the mortgage with dollar income; but the British are nothing if not flexible.)

PROFITING FROM INTEREST RATE DIFFERENTIALS

Some banks inside Britain and on the Continent offer overseas investors the right to deposit a sum in a high-yield currency and simultaneously borrow the equivalent value or more (up to four times as much, for example, in Jyske Bank in Copenhagen, Denmark) in a low-yield currency (such as the dollar or the German mark). Then you deposit the proceeds of the loan, too.

The difference between the yield and what you pay to borrow is credited to your account, which means that you can get very high interest indeed. Of course, you also are taking an exchange risk; the interest rate is higher on the second currency precisely because there is a devaluation risk.

If you cover the exchange risk by using futures, you will lose the interest advantage (because futures reflect interest rate differentials and because, for small sums, you also will have significant transaction expenses). So the only way you will come out ahead is if you can predict currency trends more successfully than can the market. You can play this game with Invest-Loan, the Jyske Bank scheme, Vesterbrogade 9, 1501 Copenhagen V, Denmark; tel. (45-31) 21-22-22.

Because Denmark is part of the Common Market, yet closely linked to the Scandinavian currency group, its currency is frequently under pressure. That is why interest rates have to be so high. For most of the past 20 years, the threatened devaluations did not cost Invest-Loan players as much money as they made by the scheme. Another scheme enables businesses to borrow against their own deposits, effectively cutting their taxable earnings and enabling them to build up assets in foreign exchange as they repay their loan. These complicated schemes are offered by banks in Britain and other haven countries. The advantage of doing them in Britain is probably that they can be explained to you more clearly there. Do get a second opinion from an accountant or tax planner. (Just because something is a way to escape taxes does not mean it makes sense for every client.)

BRITISH BANKS

- Abbey National, 219 Baker St., Abbey House, London NW1 6XL; tel. (44-71) 486-5555
- Bank of Scotland, 38 Threadneedle St., London EC2B 2BB; for "The Number One Savings Scheme": 26A York Pl., Edinburgh EH1 3EY; tel. (44-31) 442-7777; fax (44-31) 556-7390
- Barclays, 54 Lombard St., London EC3P 3AH; tel. (44-71) 626-1567
- Lloyds, 71 Lombard St., London EC3P 3BS; tel. (44-71) 248-9822; fax (44-71) 248-2361
- Midland Bank-Head Office, Poultry, London EC2P 2BX; tel. (44-71) 260-8000; fax (44-71) 260-7065
- National Westminister, 41 Lothbury, London EC2P 2BB; tel. (44-71) 606-6060; fax (44-71) 606-7273
- Royal Bank of Scotland, 142-144 Princes Square St., Edinburgh EH2 4EQ; 63 Wall St., New York, NY 10005; (212) 269-1700; fax (212) 269-8929; or 67 Lombard St., London EC3 P3QL; tel. (44-71) 623-4356

MORTGAGE COMPANIES

- Chemical Bank, Chemical Bank House, 180 Strand,

London WC2 RSlEX; tel. (44-71) 379-7474
- Coutts & Co., 27 Bush Ln., Cannon St., London EC4R OAA; tel. (44-71) 623-9661; fax (44-71) 623-1185

BUILDING SOCIETIES

- Catholic Building Society, 7 Strutton Grounds, Westminster, SW1 P24HY London; tel. (44-71) 222-6737 (Catholic Church-related, but accepts other customers)
- Nottingham Building Society, 5-13 Upper Parliament St., Nottingham NG1 2BX; tel. (44-602) 481-444; fax (44-602) 483-948

CHAPTER 8

THE BRITISH ISLES

Although you can operate an offshore bank and investment account from Britain without leaving the mainland, Britain also offers such services, often more sophisticated than those found on the mainland, from a number of islands off its coasts. For tourists, investors, and businessmen, these islands beckon.

For investors, there are more than 185 competing banks in the main islands, exclusive of other professional firms you would expect to see, such as investment houses, accountants, lawyers, trust companies, and insurance brokers. Residents of these islands pay tax at the rate of only 20 percent.

The Channel Islands of Jersey and Guernsey offer full offshore banking, trust, investment, legal, and accountancy services. There are now a small number of companies setting up on their sister island Alderney. Jersey and Guernsey earn 40 to 45 percent of their gross national product (GNP) from the financial sector, with tourism being the second biggest earner, bringing in 35 percent of the GNP.

Both islands have stiff immigration and other controls that limit the ability of banks and other financial firms that might want to move in and actually set up. Although this policy has had its critics, there is no question that the banks there represent some of the world's top institutions. There certainly is no "closed-door" policy toward companies that want to set up on the islands. This has led to the growth of banking in the less sunny climate of the Isle of Man, in the Irish Sea midway between England and Ireland.

While the offshore industry has been growing in the Channel Islands, the Isle of Man has also rapidly expanded its offshore industry. Although its financial community is smaller than its counterparts on Jersey, controls are not as strict, and it is somewhat easier for both individuals and businesses to set up there.

LONG ARM OF GOVERNMENT

For Americans, there is another consideration concerning the Channel Islands and the Isle of Man. Many of the mutual fund managers cannot sell their products in the United States because their funds have not been approved by the SEC. However, investors can still get their hands on information about these funds. You can set up an address on the islands (or anywhere else outside the United States), and have any information sent to that address. Then the materials can be forwarded to your address in the United States.

The days when most of the islands' clients were either British or expatriates are over. The banks on the three islands serve an increasingly international clientele.

CURIOUS CUSTOMS

Both Jersey and Guernsey base their laws on the customary laws of Normandy, while the Isle of Man has its own legal system and uses (in part) English common law. However, the Channel Islands have incorporated many of the principles of English common law into their commercial laws and activities.

The British Parliament has no power to pass legislation for the islands because they are not a part of the United Kingdom. Jersey and Guernsey were originally part of the

French Duchy of Normandy, and thus technically they conquered England in the year 1066. Her Majesty Queen Elizabeth II is the head of state of the islands, not as queen but in her separate title of Duchess of Normandy. The Channel Islands are the only part of the original Duchy of Normandy still under royal administration.

The only Channel Island you can easily move to is Alderney, where there is now a small number of financial service companies. There are no restrictions on rich foreign residents as there are on Jersey and, to a certain extent, Guernsey. It also is relatively easier to establish residency on the Isle of Man, which is big enough to absorb newcomers (343 square miles). It is, geographically speaking, 7 1/2 times larger than Jersey and more than 10 times bigger than Guernsey. Jersey, Guernsey, and the Isle of Man have a 20-percent income tax on residents and effectively no taxation on nonresidents who conduct their business through them.

The Channel Islands and the Isle of Man have a special relationship with the United Kingdom. They are not part of the United Kingdom, but it is responsible for their foreign relations and for the external defense of the islands. In domestic affairs, the islands virtually govern themselves, except that laws passed by their legislative assemblies must be validated by Royal Assent (but so do laws passed by the British Parliament).

The islands' relationship with the European Community (EC)—which replaced the European Economic Community (EEC) a few years ago and is itself scheduled to be replaced by the European Union (EU)—is governed by article 25-27 and Protocol 3 of the United Kingdom's Act of Accession. This protocol states that the islands are included in the EC customs territory. Goods imported to the islands from third countries are subject to the same common customs tariffs and agricultural levies as those imported into the United Kingdom. The European Commission (the governing body of the EC) also has the power to review local aid schemes to industry to ensure the maintenance of free trade.

Apart from the customs rules, the islands are excluded from the provisions of the EC treaty. The protocol stipulates, however, that although treaty provisions relating to the free movement of workers and the right of establishment do not apply to the islanders, nationals of all countries of the EC must receive identical treatment within the territories and all islanders must enjoy the same rights in the United Kingdom as UK citizens.

The islands' virtual exclusion from EC responsibilities enables them to retain proceeds from import duties and agricultural levies raised on imports from third countries from outside the EC. On the other hand, EC funds are not available to their producers, nor are compensatory amounts available for agriculture.

JERSEY

There are no party politics in Jersey, and, therefore, the tax system is not subject to manipulation for political reasons. Successive Finance Committee presidents have committed themselves to preserving the standard rate of tax, which has remained at 20 percent for more than 50 years. The possibility of any change in this rate is remote in the extreme.

Nonresidents of the island are subject to Jersey income tax only on income arising in Jersey, except with respect to interest on bank deposits, which is exempt. A local trust will be treated as nonresident for tax purposes provided that none of the beneficiaries is resident in Jersey.

GUERNSEY

Located in the English Channel but close to France and just a few miles from Jersey, Guernsey is easily accessible by sea and air and has excellent communication systems. As mentioned above, the island has a relationship with the European Community by virtue of Protocol 3 to the United Kingdom's Treaty of Accession, and it benefits greatly from the free trade association without being under an obligation to harmonize its laws or taxes. The historical, legal, and tax situations are almost identical to Jersey's.

THE ISLE OF MAN

Although the historical and legal situation is somewhat different from that of the Channel Islands, the advantages to the offshore user are very similar.

The Isle of Man has introduced new measures to protect investors. Under the 1988 Financial Supervision Act, managers of any investment scheme, a bank, a mutual fund, an insurance company, or a pension plan must be established either in the Isle or in a jurisdiction with a recognized supervisory system (which means Britain). It will no longer be possible to hide the principals of a fund management or banking group behind an anonymous corporation or trust, Manx or other.

All three islands take great care to ensure that they are not used by those whose business would cause trouble and cause the islands to lose their enviable reputations. To safeguard this, there is investor legislation in place that is every bit as tight, if not tighter, than exists in Britain. There is legislation against drug money offenses and anything that smells even remotely like money laundering.

One of the reasons it is difficult to set up a business in these centers is the stringent checks that any such businesses have to go through to make sure they meet the strict criteria set by the authorities. These authorities meet regularly, and although there are differences in emphasis among the islands (the Isle of Man has a deposit insurance plan, whereas the other two do not), the overall policy is to keep the three centers firmly in the forefront of developments in the offshore banking industry.

This does not mean that the islands jump on everything adopted by other offshore financial centers. For example, there is no desire to reproduce the International Business

Companies (IBC) legislation of the Caribbean jurisdictions. (An IBC is a form of instant company that some countries have created and are usually exempt from ordinary reporting requirements.) The likelihood that the islands will pass fraudulent-dispositions legislation of the type used in some of the Caribbean territories, Gibraltar, and the Cook Islands is small.

The islands are not part of the European Union and, therefore, not directly affected by the directives of the Eurocrats in Brussels. Because of this status, EU policies requiring member countries to harmonize their tax and company laws do not apply to these islands.

The separate legal systems of the British offshore islands is why debtors' prisons still exist and why the intersection of EC and island law often is so useful and interesting. The Isle of Man has been in dispute with the European Court of Human Rights for some years over the island's traditional punishment of birching for certain moderate offenses committed by males between ages 14 and 21. It is the only part of the United Kingdom that still retains birching as a punishment. (Do not confuse birching with the traditional English schoolboy punishment of caning that you see in so many British movies. The birch is a bundle of 15 to 20 flexible canes tied together and is definitely going to leave some painful marks on a bare bottom.) A bit of public drunkeness or minor vandalism by a young man will usually have the Manx magistrate sentencing him to a certain number of strokes of the birch. But it is not the alleged "victims" who are complaining; they all consider it far better than spending 10 days in jail, which would be likely for a similar offense in the United States or Great Britain. They consider the European action to be cultural interference and point out that the punishment is so humiliating (but not humiliating in the international human rights sense of the word) that repeat offenses are rare—again unlike in the United States.

Although the banks on the Channel Islands and the Isle of Man are not directly supervised by the Bank of England, in practice, the islands use exactly the same standards in supervising island banks. The reporting that has to be done by

The British Isles

these banks is, in some cases, even tougher than in the United Kingdom, and the authorities take compliance with these rules very seriously.

BANKING SOPHISTICATION

All this archaic judicial nonsense does not mean that British offshore island banking is medieval, unsophisticated, or insignificant. In mid-1992, total deposits in the Isle of Man banking system reached £10 billion; the total in Guernsey's 52 banks topped £17 billion; the total in Jersey was well over £45 billion. The majority of these deposits are in currencies other than sterling, particularly on Jersey and Guernsey, emphasizing the truly international nature of business carried out through the islands.

At one time, the main business of Guernsey, Jersey, and the Isle of Man was operating funds for Britons who did not live in their country because of jobs, tax avoidance, or retirement. However, this is no longer true.

Although there was a tendency at one time for the islands to be administrative centers for business, with the major decisions on policy and strategy carried out on the mainland, this is generally no longer the case. The very high level of professional standards and the number of diverse professionals ensure that virtually every type of business is genuinely carried out on the islands. The major financial centers are only used when they have to be.

The investment industry, for example, has come into its own with substantial funds managed on the islands, £10 billion on Jersey alone. There are a number of major stockbrokerages, such as Le Masurier James & Chinn, that are part of the Banque Indosuez Group and manage, deal, and advise on Jersey. They are, however, linked to an international network, with all the benefits that it brings. Jersey also has other UK stockbrokerages, such as James Capel and Quilter Goodison. N.M. Rothchilds and other large banks, such as Coutts & Company, are present as well.

There are no agreements that prohibit banks on any of the islands from offering their services to nationals of any country, especially from pressure applied by another country's government. It is true that Jersey did not encourage British building societies and banks on the island to take deposits from British nationals, who wanted to have their interest payments paid gross as opposed to net in the United Kingdom. This, however, was an island decision. Jersey did not want to be seen as offering services that might be taken as blatantly encouraging tax evasion. However, if any British person came to the island in order to open such an account, he would not be turned away.

As with any major bank in an offshore financial center—and this applies to all such centers— there is always the possibility that the authorities seeking information will put pressure on the parent nation to get the information from the offshore banking center.

Generally, no banks or services will divulge any information merely because they have been asked for it. They will do so only if a court order has been served on them and only if that court order came from an island court. Aside from money laundering, drugs, or crime, such orders will usually only be issued for fraudulent transactions. For example, they will not assist another authority in the prosecution of a tax debt; if Mr. Doe owes taxes in the United States, the islands will not assist the IRS in getting the revenue.

It is particularly important when opening an account in a "suspect" site (and any English-speaking offshore banking haven is suspect) to make sure that you are not leaping from the frying pan into the fire. We will discuss the case of Standard Chartered in New York and Bank Leu in the Bahamas later. The U.S. courts will stop at nothing to induce banks with operations in the United States to give them information about offshore clients.

A way around the problem is to use a bank that does not operate in the United States, although the number is very small. Most of the banks on the islands are major financial institutions that are widely spread throughout the world. On the Isle of Man, Duncan Lawrie is therefore a better idea than institutions affiliated with large British commercial banks with U.S. operations. Their address is Duncan Lawrie, 14/15 Mount Havelock, Douglas, Isle of Man; tel. (44-624) 620770, fax (44-624) 676315; contact Mr. Bruce Dutton, Director. On Jersey, there are two banks that do not have any U.S. affiliation. One is Cater Allan (Jersey), Ltd. The other bank is Standard Bank Investment Corporation, Ltd. Both are in St. Helier.

AMERICAN AMBIVALENCE

Fund management services are not only for corporations, insurance companies, and the rich. They also are for ordinary middle-class investors. They typically include free switching worldwide between funds that invest in Britain—or in money market instruments in sterling or other currencies.

If you try to buy shares in a British offshore (Channel Islands) fund, however, you will be required to sign a declaration something like this one:

> I/We declare that the shares are not being acquired directly or indirectly by a U.S. person nor in violation of any applicable law. A "U.S. Person" includes a national or resident of the United States of America, a partnership organized or existing in any state, territory or possession of the United States of America, a corporation organized under the laws of the United States of America or of any state, territory, or possession thereof, or any estate or trust, other than an estate or trust the income of which comes from sources outside the United States of America (which is not effectively connected with conduct of a trade or business within the United States

of America) or is not included in gross income for the purposes of computing United States federal income tax. For the purposes of this definition, "United States of America" includes the United States of America, its territories and possessions and areas subject to its jurisdiction.

Most of these mutual-fund groups will not even mail their literature to a U.S. address because they are not registered with the SEC and therefore do not sell their funds to U.S. citizens.

A few Channel Islands unit trust groups, such as Lloyd's Bank in Jersey or Rothschilds, interpret the SEC laws differently, and they will accept your investment, even by mail. However, they do try to organize things so that their canvassing letters are not sent wholesale to the United States. You will also find a large number of portfolio management companies willing to accept your money because they are stock-exchange-listed in London and therefore don't need to be registered in the United States as well.

The Channel Islands are the preferred place for offshore money-market funds for the British expatriate market. Because of a legal quirk, this once was the only place where a single corporate entity could offer money-market funds operating in a variety of currencies, making it easier for funds to offer free switching between currencies to customers investing only modest sums.

Other offshore centers now offer streamlined incorporation, but the Channel Islands remain the center for multicurrency money-market and bond funds. Given the British coloration of the islands, sterling-denominated funds are the most popular single currency. As of this writing, Jersey managers run over £800 million in gilt funds invested in British treasury bonds.

The range of business being conducted on the Channel Islands and the Isle of Man is becoming increasingly diverse. Apart from the various mutual funds set up for entities throughout the world—from South Korea and Japan to North and South America—all other business is equally diverse. Many employee-benefits programs are run from the islands, especially on Jersey, where one company, Mourant & Company, has carved a niche for itself. Major corporate business involving debt defeasance and securitization plans, financial restructuring, stock and bond issues, captive insurance programs, and leasing can all be done on the islands. Much of this revolves around the trusts and companies set up under the laws of the three islands, where the legal practices, accountancy firms, and their specialized trust companies play a major role.

Equally diverse is the range of private client business being carried out. Hong Kong Chinese who are immigrating to North America work out their financial affairs through the islands. The Gulf War gave a major impetus to business from investors worried about the safety of their assets—there are few places in the world more politically stable than these islands. Wherever there are exchange controls, there will be citizens of those countries setting up vehicles on the islands to ensure that their external assets are kept out of the clutches of their home authorities.

Whereas many of these plans involve assets of considerable size, the islands also deal with a substantial client base where the sums are at the bottom of the range. The sophisticated vehicles used for the wealthy are generally not available to the smaller client because the costs would outweigh the benefits to them. However, in such cases, there are often alternatives that can be set up that do not charge enormous fees.

The Channel Islands and the Isle of Man have an enviable reputation. They are not in the same league as some jurisdictions that encourage business without knowing what the business is. There are strict guidelines and, in some areas, laws as to what can and cannot be done, but this only reinforces the reputations of the islands and, therefore, the investors and clients whom they serve.

BRITISH ISLES BANKS

- Framlington Overseas Fund Management Ltd., Barfield House, St. Julian's Ave., Guernsey, C.I.; tel. (44-481) 726541; fax (44-481) 714450
- Gartmore Fund Managers International Ltd. (Banque Indosuez of France), P.O. Box 278, 45 La Motte St., St. Helier, Jersey, C.I.; tel. (44-534) 27301
- Guiness Flight Fund Managers (Guernsey) Ltd., P.O. Box 188, St. Peter Port, Guernsey, C.I.; tel. (44-481) 723506
- Hambros Fund Managers (Channel Islands) Ltd., P.O. Box 6, St. Julians Ave., St. Peter Port, Guernsey, C.I.; tel. (44-481) 715454; fax (44-481) 715299
- Hill Samuel Investors (Channel Islands) Ltd., P.O. Box 63, 7 Bond St., St. Helier, Jersey, C.I.; tel. (44-534) 73244; fax (44-534) 79018/69800
- Isle of Man Bank, 6062 Athol St., Douglas, Isle of Man; tel. (44-624) 29521 (National Westminster-linked)
- John Govett Management Ltd., P.O. Box 208, St. Peter Port, Guernsey, C.I.; tel. (44-481) 26268
- Rothschild Asset Management, P.O. Box 58, St. Julians Court, St. Peter Port, Guernsey, C.I.; tel. (44-481) 713713; fax (44-481) 712575
- Royal Bank of Canada (Channel Islands) Ltd., P.O. Box 48, St. Peter Port, Guernsey, C.I.; tel. (44-481) 723021; fax (44-481) 723524

CHAPTER 9

THE CAYMAN ISLANDS

The Cayman Islands are hardly bigger than a speck on the map—except in banking. There are 538 licensed banks, including 44 of the 50 largest in the world. They hold about $250 billion in foreign assets. The Cayman advantage for banking is an almost unique combination of banking secrecy and regulation against fraud and suspect money. There are many banking havens in warm waters off the shores of the United States, but few are as appealing.

The Caymans comprise three islands 450 miles south of Florida. They are a British Crown Colony. Not one is seeking independence. The largest island (where Columbus landed) is called Grand Cayman and is the site of the capital, Georgetown. The government is committed to keeping a financial industry going based on no taxation.

The natives, who are racially mixed, are very devout and hardworking. Before banking got going in the mid-1960s, they were famous in the world of shipping as navigators for huge oil tankers.

Big banks from the United States, Switzerland, and Britain are among the licensed banks of Cayman. Because U.S. banks often maintain copies of their Cayman Islands records on their computers in the United States, a foreign bank is probably preferable.

Regulation is tight and banking licenses are not easy to come by. When political problems arose in Panama in 1988, many disreputable banks that tried to flee to Cayman found the door shut. Under the 1986 Mutual Assistance Pact with the United States and other banking centers, only clean money was welcome.

Major banks on the island include Barclays and National Westminster of Britain, Bank Julius Baer of Zurich, Canadian Imperial Bank, Royal Bank of Canada, and Bank of Nova Scotia from Canada. All of these have U.S. branches or subsidiaries, and all would provide information to the U.S. authorities in the event of a serious charge of money laundering.

A better bet might be N.T. Butterfield & Son in Georgetown, which is a subsidiary of a bank in Bermuda. Nicholas Duggan, who heads that bank, is current president of the Cayman Islands Bankers' Association, presumably a mark of peer respect. Butterfield recently opened another offshore bank in the Channel Islands, in Guernsey.

Bank of Bermuda also operates in Cayman and Guernsey; however, it also has a subsidiary in New York City. Banking products available in Cayman run the gamut from CDs to money-market accounts, from mutual funds to fiduciary services, from company formation to foreign exchange. Asset management for high-net-worth individuals is growing, and more and more portfolio management is being done right on the island, rather than from a faraway base.

U.S. ASSAULT ON BANKING PRIVACY

U.S. regulators are making waves in the Caribbean, so much so that some of the islands fear they will be swamped. Since 1982, pressure from their neighbor to the north has led offshore tax haven countries in the Caribbean to relax bank secrecy and agree to exchange tax information with the United States. Sometimes these countries are promised U.S. aid in return.

Among the countries that have given in to pressure are Panama, the Bahamas, the Dutch Antilles, the Cayman Islands, Bermuda, and the Turks and Caicos Islands. In 1987, the U.S. Treasury attempted to crack down on U.S. corporate use of Netherlands Antilles subsidiaries to raise money on the Euromarkets.

Even the Caymans—which are on the other side of Cuba from Key West—signed a treaty with the United States giving the authorities wide access to the financial records of Cayman banks in criminal investigations. The June 1986 agreement provides that the Attorney General of the Cayman Islands may order disclosure of confidential banking and corporate information to U.S. officials investigating matters that would constitute criminal activity in the Cayman Islands.

The U.S. authorities do not have to obtain a court order in the Caymans to look at banking or corporate records. They only need to show to the satisfaction of the Cayman Attorney General that the information being sought is relevant to a criminal investigation. Tax evasion arising out of drug trafficking is specifically included.

The heat is on—and not just from the sun. As a result, there has been considerable movement out of the islands and into other havens, notably Switzerland. The most recent figures of the Swiss National Bank show that enormous sums flowed from sunny places into their banking system last year: SFr 6.08 billion (US$4.07 billion) from the Cayman Islands, SFr 7.67 billion (US$5.14 billion) from the Bahamas, and SFr 8.9 billion (US$5.96 billion) from Panama (U.S. conversions based on rate of 1.5 SFr per U.S. dollar, the value given in *USA Today*, November 18, 1993). Because these sites are used to create trusts, some of this money may not be fleeing the Caribbean but merely flowing through it.

LESS CARIBBEAN VULNERABILITY

Nonetheless, the British-owned Cayman Islands are less susceptible to pressure from their big neighbor to the north than are other banking havens. First of all, they are not independent. For this reason, the inflow of money from the United States cannot easily be tracked statistically. Second, they are not asking for aid under the Caribbean Initiative and other programs—which come with strings attached. Last, the U.S. Treasury's own report on crackdowns on tax evasion (before the new agreement was in effect) showed that the Cayman Islands were less likely to be used to hide drug money than were other banking havens in the Caribbean, such as Panama and the Bahamas.

SUNSHINE AND BANKING

The Caymans have a number of advantages in the haven business. One is convenience. The islands are a short hop by plane from Miami, Houston, or Atlanta. You can combine banking with tourism, which has developed almost as rapidly. The Seven-Mile Beach on Grand Cayman, for example, is a popular tourist destination. There are no exchange controls. You can direct dial from the United States by telephone. The Caymans are in the Eastern Standard Time zone.

Under the 1976 Confidential Relationship Law, it is a criminal offense for any person to divulge information provided during the course of business under conditions of express or implied confidentially. The punishment is a fine that is doubled if the violator is a professional—and quadrupled if he answered in response to a bribe.

One bank on the island boasts that it offers a gold MasterCard processed by Caymanians in the Caymans. Such a card gives you access to your money in the United States and 140 other countries—without leaving any traces because the identity of the cardholder is known only to the administration of the bank, which is subject to the Caymanian secrecy law. For this service, you have to contact a bank that has no branches or affiliates outside the island, Finsbury Bank and Trust, Transnational House, West Bay Road, P.O. Box

The Cayman Islands 81

1592, Grand Cayman, B.W.I.; tel. (809) 947-4011; fax (809) 947-4650; contact John Johnson. Banking regulation is by the Cayman Islands Inspector of Banks, overseen by the Governor General (appointed by the Queen of England) and the popularly elected legislature. Only class A banks, which have a high capital requirement, may take deposits. Class B banks of the Islands may only operate offshore from the Caymans. Moreover, they must be located in and use the administrative support of class A banks. This enables some control over their activities, as well as their being subject to supervision by the Cayman banking inspectors. All the banks listed at the end of this chapter are either class A or class B banks.

BRITISH VIRGIN ISLANDS

The British Virgin Islands (BVI) are getting set to become a major rival to Grand Cayman. They too benefit from being Crown possessions—and they are better able to dodge pressures from their big neighbors to the north than are independent countries receiving American aid.

The BVI, which are even smaller than the Caymans (56 square miles of territory and 12,000 inhabitants), currently have just four banks: Chase, Barclays, Scotiabank of Canada, and First Pennsylvania. BVI law allows the cheap formation of a company that can hold assets or executive transactions. Only major international banks can receive banking licenses. BVI registration provides secrecy because the identity of owners is shielded. Also, there is no income tax on these international business companies.

The ordinary companies law, which was in effect before this special international business companies law, is still in effect. Sometimes formation of a company under this law is more useful, particularly if one wants to take advantage of the double tax treaties still in effect with Japan and Switzerland.

BVI used to have a double-tax treaty with the United States, but we canceled it a decade ago. BVI companies must now pay withholding tax on receipts of interest and dividends from the United States.

After the demise of the treaty, the 1984 International Business Companies Ordinance was put into place. The new law led to ballooning registration of companies, which numbered fewer than 1,000 when the law was passed. There are now more than 60,000 companies registered in the BVI.

OTHER HAVENS IN THE WESTERN HEMISPHERE

The Bahamas
These islands are home to hundreds of international banks, most operating "brass plate" establishments on Bay Street. Few banks are able to avoid pressure being brought on their U.S. branches, however.

Bermuda
Other options are Bermuda banks that operate only in offshore bank havens: Butterfield Bank, in particular (see above under Cayman Islands). The larger Bank of Bermuda is 100 years old and has $5 billion in assets. However, in addition to offices in the Cayman Islands, Guernsey, Hong Kong, the Isle of Man, and Luxembourg, it has a subsidiary in New York.

Turks and Caicos Islands
Just south of the Bahamas, these islands have their own legislation to attract offshore business and permit the formation of trusts. They want to become "the Liechtenstein of the Western Hemisphere by the year 2000," Finance Minister Oswald Skippings says. Five banks now have licenses, with Barclays, Scotiabank, and Toronto-Dominion being the best known. The British government has removed the moratorium on granting new banks the right to open.

The trust law provides for privacy and no requirement that the trust be registered with the government. The beneficial owners' names need not be revealed. However, the islands will not allow "fraudulent settlements" and will cooperate to stop fraud. Business people using the islands will be subject to background checks from the FBI and INTERPOL to try to stop dirty money. (In 1985, three Turks and Caicos officials, including the then chief minister, were arrested in Miami, convicted of drug trafficking, and sentenced to eight years in U.S. federal prison.)

Anguilla
Anguilla is a British colony. Once the home of numerous dubious banks, the fraud squad from London came in and cleaned house, and the bank charters have all been revoked. Money laundering of the proceeds of drug smuggling is said to be still taking place.

Montserrat
This is an even more disreputable banking center, where hanky-panky involving banks appealing to British expatriates and bank scandals are reported.

Panama
Panama's banking sector is attempting to revive since the U.S. invasion. Bankers are anxious to reassert the sanctity of banking secrecy legislation despite the collection by U.S. occupation troops and American agents of material regarding financial operations by Manuel Noriega and members of his former regime. Offshore banking and incorporation was a major source of revenues for the country in the past, and the economic revival of Panama, it can be argued, depends on reestablishing facilities with safeguards sufficient to ensure that abuses do not recur. The banking haven business has always been auxiliary to the more substantial and legitimate use of Panama for tax haven trading companies, the use of the free zone at the end of the Panama Canal, and headquarters for many regional sales subsidiaries of world class corporations.

Puerto Rico

Another Caribbean island offering offshore banking services is rather astonishing: Puerto Rico, which is a U.S. commonwealth and therefore is discussed in our U.S. chapter.

CAYMAN ISLANDS BANKS

- BankAmerica Trust & Banking Corp. (Cayman) Ltd., P.O. Box 1092, Grand Cayman, BWI; tel. (809) 949-7888; fax (809) 949-7883; contact Charles Farrington
- Cayman National Bank & Trust Co., P.O. Box 1097, Grand Cayman, BWI; tel. (809) 949-4655; fax (809) 949-7506 (Cayman National has recently issued its own MasterCard)
- Cayman Securities Ltd., P.O. Box 275, Grand Cayman, BWI; tel. (809) 949-7722; fax (809) 949-8203; contact Dan Maristick
- Ansbacher Corp., P.O. Box 887, Grand Cayman, BWI; tel. (809) 949-4653; fax (809) 949-7946
- Midland Bank Trust Corp. (Cayman) Ltd., P.O. Box 1109, Mary Street and Fort Street, Georgetown, Grand Cayman, BWI; tel. (809) 949-7755; fax (809) 949-7634
- MIM Britannia International Investments Ltd., P.O. Box 609, Grand Cayman, BWI; tel. (809) 949-8144; fax (809) 949-7761
- Swiss Bank & Trust Corp. Ltd., Swiss Bank Bldg., P.O. Box 852, Georgetown, Grand Cayman, BWI; tel. (809) 949-7344; fax (809) 949-7308
- Overland Bank, P.O. Box 1792, Anderson Sq., Georgetown, Grand Cayman, BWI; tel. (809) 949-8721; fax (809) 949-7946.

CHAPTER 10
HONG KONG

There is a cloud hanging over Hong Kong—1997. In that year the island reverts to China. Many of the best bankers in the colony are trying to establish their own futures elsewhere before the boom falls. Britain, which held the lease, allowed the whole colony to revert and then failed to allow the influx of those of the island's citizenry who prefer to live under capitalism.

However, China has made huge financial investments in Hong Kong. It holds substantial interests in real estate (the state-owned Bank of China is one of the tallest in Asia) and has acquired significant shares in major Hong Kong companies. The People's Republic of China appears to have a vested interest in keeping Hong Kong's economic engine in fine tune.

Another frustration is the way the SEC has failed to respect what tenuous claims to sovereignty the little island may possess. (The assault is described in the chapter on the United States.)

The U.S. government has taken the lead in trying to pry open bank secrecy. For example, the U.S. Justice Department has demanded from Barclays Bank in Hong Kong details of an account said to belong to Ferdinand Marcos. Under normal circumstances (not involving fraud), the fluid Hong Kong banking ordinance does not allow bank regulators in the colony to give information about an individual customer's affairs to overseas supervisory authorities. This is the same law that is applied in Britain. But Hong Kong does not have a banking secrecy law, such as the Caymans or Switzerland has.

A very few banks will still open an account without a signature. To open such an account, you do not have to fill out a signature card, but rather have a "chop" made, a Chinese seal, that the bank will accept for identification. This is widely discouraged and not done by most banks. Usually the service is only available if you are an elderly, respected, and well-known Chinese gentleman.

Because Hong Kong is a major stock market and futures and currencies center, financial operations there can be carried out with a degree of sophistication not always possible from other centers. Furthermore, fund management is carried out right in Hong Kong—not in some faraway site. Fund managers, analysts, and traders are in close contact with functioning local and international markets. When markets close, however, as they did for four days in the wake of the Wall Street crash in October 1987, Hong Kong operations in commodities, futures, and currencies got caught in the panic.

Hong Kong's reputation as a free-for-all market was fed by the lack of serious obstacles to insider trading, self-dealing, and other practices that would land people in jail in other countries. One bank that failed lent most of its deposits to associated companies. These laws have been severely tightened in recent years, and local regulators are trying hard to meet world standards.

A HAVEN'S HAVEN: MACAU

An hour from Hong Kong by hydrofoil is another budding haven, Macau. The Macau Issuing Institute (something like a central bank) is planning to cash in on the effect of new Hong Kong banking rules. Offshore banking units set up under Macau law and subject to moderate taxation will be exempt from liquidity ratios. They will also be exempt from rules limiting the amount they may lend to any one borrower (as long as it is less than one-third of their capital).

Thus far, only one Portuguese bank has created an offshore banking unit. By holding out the possibility of locating house banks there, Macau is proposing to become an offshore center for another offshore center, Hong Kong. (There are now 23 banks in Macau, including international biggies, but most of them have trouble with the lack of infrastructure and trained staff.)

COMMUNIST SECRECY

For those who are not overseas Chinese, probably the best place for an account is the Hong Kong branch of the Bank of Communications, headquartered in Beijing, China. The Chinese are theoretically committed to maintaining Hong Kong's stock market, banks, and financial independence for 50 years after the crown colony reverts to China.

The advantage of Bank of Communications is that, unlike the Bank of China, it does not have a U.S. branch subject to the kind of pressures that were brought against Standard Chartered. Beware of Hong Kong's best-known bank, Hongkong & Shanghai Banking Corp. Thanks to its purchase of Marine Midland, a New York bank (as part of its diversification away from the potentially Communist crown colony), it too can be pressured by American authorities.

One can expect the Hong Kong branch of the Bank of Communications to resist any pressure from the United States to lift bank secrecy practices. There are U.S. banks in Hong Kong. If you open an account there, you will be asked to sign a waiver allowing secrecy to be lifted at the request of U.S. authorities. That is a good argument for going Communist or at least non-American.

HONG KONG BANKS

- Bank of Communications, Hong Kong Branch, Wheelock House, Central, Hong Kong; tel. (852) 841-9611; fax (852) 810-6993
- Hongkong & Shanghai Banking Corp., 1 Queens Rd., Central, Hong Kong; tel. (852) 822-1111; fax (852) 868-1646
- Jardine Fleming, 46th Floor, Jardine House, Central, Hong Kong; tel. (852) 843-8888; fax (852) 845-0468
- KB International (Hong Kong) Ltd., Bond Center Tower, 89 Queensway, Central, Hong Kong (Luxembourg parent); tel. (852) 868-3191; fax (852) 868-5415
- Rabobank, 2 Exchange Sq., 16/F, 8 Connaught Bank Bldg., Central, Hong Kong; tel. (852) 526-3249; fax (852) 868-5915
- Royal Trust Asia Ltd., 32/F One Exchange Sq., 8 Connaught Pl., Hong Kong; tel. (852) 847-8606. U.S. contact: James Therrian, Royal Trust International, 1420 Fifth Ave., Suite 2200, Seattle, WA 98101; tel. (206) 224-3210, fax (206) 224-3575
- Wardley Ltd., Hutchison House, 7th Floor, 10 Harcourt Rd., Hong Kong; tel. (852) 841-8888; fax (852) 520-2517
- Yamaichi Securities Co. Ltd., 12th Floor, Hutchison House, Central, Hong Kong; tel. (852) 524-8014; fax (852) 845-3534

CHAPTER 11

SWITZERLAND

It may seem odd to wait until now to discuss what most people assume is the most popular location for foreign bank accounts. There are good reasons. One is that Switzerland is a red flag to the authorities of other countries looking for tax evaders. Fortunately, the United States cannot go as far as neighboring France—whose customs officials record the license numbers of French-registered automobiles in Geneva. They then send orders back to the frontier to stop and search the car when it returns to France.

Heaven help the Frenchman who left a Swiss bank paper on his dashboard or in his glove compartment. The French also systematically screen mail to and from Switzerland for magnetically stripped checks. Not long ago, two French officials were arrested for bribing a Swiss bank employee to provide computer tapes of client account data. All three were locked up by the Swiss. The accounts were nominal—not the famous Swiss numbered accounts.

Although the United States may be somewhat less zealous than the French, there are rumors that U.S. nationals who visit Switzerland too often may be subject to tax audits. U.S. citizens receiving too much mail from Switzerland may also be similarly scrutinized.

WITHHOLDING TAX

The Swiss impose a 35-percent withholding tax on interest paid by a Swiss payor. You can recover this money by the simple expedient of declaring the interest to the IRS. You can either obtain a refund from the Swiss, after getting the proper forms certified by the IRS, or you can apply the amount as a credit on your U.S. taxes under the foreign tax credit rules. Note that this is a credit, not a deduction, so it comes right off the amount of the check you would have paid to the IRS. However, the Swiss do not issue 1099 forms, and it may be difficult to determine the appropriate exchange rate for the dollar, although the IRS eventually gets around to printing an official rate for the preceding year.

One way to avoid the withholding tax is to have a fiduciary account instead of a regular bank account. This is really the equivalent of having the trust department of an American bank handle your investments for you instead of putting the money in a CD. More information on fiduciary accounts is given in the Swiss bank services section. All the investments are made outside Switzerland, in whatever you tell the bank to do—mortgages, mutual funds, other banks. The money is merely passing through Switzerland and is not taxed there.

SECRECY UNDER ASSAULT

Another problem is that Swiss bank secrecy is not as solid as it used to be. A few years ago, the Swiss banking secrecy law protected Marc Rich, who had violated U.S. laws (but not Swiss ones). Things have changed a lot since then. Both Imelda Marcos and Baby Doc Duvalier probably wish that they had not assumed that their Swiss bank deposits were untraceable.

The United States is believed to be responsible for the Swiss change of heart over the accounts of Marcos and

Duvalier (to say nothing of Colonel North). In another recent case, Swiss banking authorities waived secrecy laws to expose a Frenchman who had been trading on Wall Street using tips he had received from an American relative. He had used Union Bank of Switzerland in Zurich to make the trades.

Furthermore, insider trading is illegal under Swiss law. Swiss experts believe that it is pressure from the SEC rather than concern for their own stock markets that led to this change in the law. With insider trading made a crime in Switzerland, bank secrecy can be lifted in response to foreign courts investigating transactions on their markets that may indicate misuse of confidential information.

Already Switzerland and the United States have exchanged "diplomatic notes" on information sharing in cases of illegal insider trading. In fact, the Swiss have cooperated with the SEC on this matter since an "understanding" was signed in 1982.

Swiss banking is often identified in America with banking secrecy. Popular media stories have created two contradictory pictures: that Swiss secrecy hinders law enforcement officers from prosecuting criminals, or that Swiss secrecy does not exist anymore and is as full of holes as a Swiss cheese. Neither is true.

The basic position in Swiss civil law is that the information concerning a customer and the customer's financial dealings is protected as part of the individual's legal right to privacy. In Switzerland, this has been made part of Article 28 of the Swiss Civil Code and not only protects the information, but makes the person violating the secrecy liable to pay damages to the customer. In addition, the banking law makes it a criminal offense in Switzerland for a banker to divulge information about a customer in violation of the law, punishable by fine or imprisonment. Both the bank and the bank employee may be subject to various penalties if a violation occurs.

A bank can only disclose information when authorized to do so under existing statutory provisions or by a Swiss court order, which must be founded on law. Secrecy is interpreted so broadly that it is illegal for a bank to say whether or not a person is a customer since, if the bank failed to do so, it would be implying that the person was a customer.

The right of secrecy is a right belonging to the customer, not the bank. It is the customer's privacy that is protected by law. The customer can waive the secrecy, but the bank cannot. For example, the customer may waive secrecy and ask the bank to give a credit reference to a specific creditor. But such a waiver is only valid if the customer acts voluntarily and not under duress. Therefore, waivers that were signed pursuant to foreign court orders compelling a customer to sign a waiver may well be invalid.

A financial institution cannot ask the government for an order waiving secrecy. Only the customer can waive the secrecy.

Contrary to an opinion current in America, Swiss secrecy is not absolute. It can be overridden by statutory provisions that compel the giving of information.

Such rules requiring disclosure of information—usually with a limited scope—can be found in Swiss inheritance law (you really wouldn't want your legitimate heir going into the insurance company with your death certificate to be told it can't tell him anything), in enforcement of judgments from creditors, in bankruptcy, or in divorce.

The most widely known limitation on secrecy is in treaties concerning Swiss cooperation in foreign criminal matters. In a criminal investigation conducted in Switzerland of a Swiss crime committed by a Swiss citizen, secrecy can be lifted by court order. The treaties extend this possibility to foreign crimes by foreign citizens in foreign investigations, but only in the limited circumstances spelled out in the treaties.

Before a foreign legal assistance request for Swiss financial records can be honored, the following conditions must be met:

1. Compulsory disclosure is only possible if the offense

that is being prosecuted is punishable as a criminal offense in both countries (the requesting state and Switzerland).

2. In tax cases, assistance is available to foreign prosecutors only if the investigated violation of foreign tax laws would be qualified under Swiss law as a tax fraud and not merely as tax evasion. Tax evasion is simply the failure to declare income or assets for taxation. Tax fraud is distinguished by the fact that "fraudulent conduct" is involved. Normally fraudulent conduct can only be assumed if forged documents are used.

There is a special provision of the Swiss-U.S. Treaty on Mutual Assistance in Criminal Matters that provides Swiss legal assistance to U.S. prosecutors even in tax evasion cases if they are conducting an investigation against an organized crime group.

3. As a general rule, the information obtained in Switzerland through a legal assistance procedure may not be used for investigative purposes nor be introduced into evidence in the requesting state in any proceeding relating to an offense other than the offense for which assistance has been granted.

It must be emphasized that foreign authorities or foreign courts cannot directly ask a Swiss financial institution for information. Even in cases in which legal assistance can be granted and therefore secrecy is lifted, only a Swiss court order—which in these cases is based on a foreign request for legal assistance—can validly lift secrecy.

Considering this, it can be said that secrecy is strict and is only put aside in case clearly defined by Swiss law and pursuant to Swiss rules. Secrecy is, however, not absolute and does therefore not protect criminals.

Switzerland has long served as a magnet for the money of wealthy foreigners who perceive the world as buffeted by overtaxation, over-regulation, and political turmoil. They are attracted, of course, by the confidentiality and discretion that have been a hallmark of Swiss bankers since the French Revolution, when they offered financial refuge to French aristocrats. In 1934 secrecy was enshrined into law.

NEW REGULATIONS

Switzerland has imposed new regulations requiring that lawyers give clients' names when making deposits on their behalf. Specifically, the lawyers must either disclose their clients' identity or swear that they are not serving as asset managers. If a lawyer swore falsely, he would be liable to pursuit in court by the bank that took the deposit.

BANK NOTE BUSINESS

Although this loophole has been closed by the Swiss authorities, they are resisting other attempts to get them to regulate banks more closely. The Swiss Federal Banking Commission, for example, investigated "bank note" transactions totaling over $1 billion. (A bank note transaction is a cash transaction.) These were carried out by Union Bank of Switzerland and Credit Suisse with two Lebanese currency dealers accused of being a conduit for illegal funds from drug-ring profits.

Switzerland accounts for about 8 percent of the world trade in bank notes. The two alleged money launderers, Lebanese brothers named Magharian, sent the bank notes into Switzerland. Two-thirds of the money was transferred to accounts in 300 banks outside the country, mostly in Turkey. The remainder was invested in precious metals.

After 15 hours of testimony from the bankers involved, the authorities issued a 28-page report saying that no additional legislation was needed. However, the report suggested that guidelines be prepared for cash transactions by the Swiss Bankers Association, an industry group. In the two banks in question, the bank note business was carried out by low-level employees who were not supervised closely because there is not much credit risk involved.

Self-regulation has therefore been determined to be sufficient for "due diligence," as required by Swiss adhesion to the UN-sponsored crackdown on money laundering of drug profits. The practical effect is that most Swiss banks retain the strong secrecy protection of the past. Only in the rare case where criminal activity under Swiss law against insider trading or accepting the profits of crime has been proven can bank secrecy be lifted.

CONFIDENTIALITY FOR LOW-PROFILE DEPOSITORS

These developments most affect politically prominent depositors. If you are not a Third World dictator or don't work in the White House, there is little reason not to open a Swiss bank account for purposes other than insider trading. Swiss bank secrecy will cover most normal uses for a foreign bank account.

Switzerland is politically stable (with a democracy that has roots in the thirteenth century), and it has been neutral in all wars since the eighteenth century. It benefits from a strong currency and a traditionally low inflation rate. Its currency tends to move with that of its most important trading partner, Germany.

Because of the appreciation of the Swiss franc over the past two decades, U.S. owners of Swiss bank accounts have made a lot of money despite the normally low interest rate, the existence of a high Swiss withholding tax, and even periods when accounts were subject to negative interest. In other words, foreigners had to pay a kind of "rent" for the privilege of keeping their money in Swiss banks.

TRADITION OF MONEY MANAGEMENT

The Swiss have been in the business of looking after other nationalities' investments since the middle of the eighteenth century when any French aristocrat worth his powdered wig had a relationship with a Swiss (probably Protestant) banker—something he must have thanked his Catholic God for in 1789 when the French Revolution broke out. Having been in the international portfolio management business for more than 200 years, the Swiss know how to do it.

Swiss banks do both investment banking and deposit-and-loan banking. They also will invest for you in Switzerland's own stock market—but there are a few problems. First of all, you will be subject to the same 35 percent withholding tax on Swiss stocks and bonds.

Another discouraging factor is how expensive some of these shares have become. Swiss law does not allow stock splits to dip below SFr 100 in the nominal (par) value of stocks. So a company that has grown to world size, such as Nestlé, cannot split its stock any further. As a result, a single share of Nestlé is worth a portfolio to most of us.

In addition, buying some shares or classes of shares in the Swiss markets is limited to Swiss nationals. Also, commissions are high because there is no competition on charges.

BEARER SHARES

It is traditional in Switzerland to use bearer shares, meaning that there is no record of who owns the stock (although the buyer bank will have to certify that the purchaser is a Swiss in some cases). The same applies to bonds.

During the past few years, many international companies incorporated in Switzerland have allowed their stockholders to register. That means, among other things, that ownership of their shares can be opened to foreigners. In addition, in cases where two classes of stock existed and registered shares were paid a higher dividend, the change has the result of making all shareholders equal. A major impetus toward the registration of bearer shares has come from the U.S.-listed closed-end fund investing in Swiss stocks and bonds, the Helvetia Fund.

BREAKING THE BROKERAGE CARTEL

The threat to Switzerland's role as a bank haven is not, as

some sensational publications would have it, the lifting of bank secrecy. It is, rather, the increasing competition to provide private banking services in that country. While some feel this threatens the profitability of small Swiss private banks organized as partnerships, most do not. Private banks are the strongest because of their reputation of putting privacy above all. In any event, these banks were required by 1992 to meet new international capital-to-asset ratios.

As has happened in the U.S. and British markets, price competition in brokerage and management services has finally come to Swiss banks, and fees are now negotiable, particularly for large accounts.

DISCRETIONARY ACCOUNTS

If you have something on the order of $100,000 to invest (depending on the bank, more at most of them), you might consider a discretionary account with a Swiss bank. The bank will manage the investment for you, according to criteria you define. The investment will move among markets and currencies and instruments, according to the bank's best judgment.

For this sort of operation, you should consider Geneva's private banks, rather than the large nationwide Swiss banks. Most of these banks require a $250,000 minimum investment. Remember that most of the smaller Swiss banks (except for Baer and Vontobel, which are listed on the Swiss stock market) do not publish their balance sheets. Many of them will not accept business without an introduction. This is not a matter for a first-time overseas investor to undertake with only a book as a guide.

The leading Swiss private banks are Pictet, Lombard Odier, and Hentsch in Geneva. (Hentsch will take an account with $100,000, but the others probably will not.) They do not welcome walk-in clients. Two other private banks are a bit more accessible: Gutzailler, because it is a Eurobond issuer, and Vontobel, because it does corporate finance. It is possible to use a corporate banking relationship as a doorway to private banking services at these banks, which is why they are included in the listings at the end of this chapter.

Swiss banks have developed the gold storage business into a fine art. Although the days of sales-tax-free gold buying in Switzerland are over, the fee for storing your gold in Switzerland is still quite low. The minimums vary from bank to bank, but many minimums are as much as one kilogram (2.2 pounds) or 30 gold coins. Banque Union de Crédit has no minimum for storage. It is perfectly legal for Americans to buy and store gold outside the United States. You do not have to declare to any authorities that you own gold abroad in any amount. However, you should declare for U.S. taxes any capital gain from a sale of gold.

Despite these options, most foreigners in Switzerland have simple bank accounts. Most of these are not numbered accounts, but ordinary name accounts. The minimums for ordinary accounts (which vary by bank) are much lower. You can arrange for your bank to keep your statements for you or send them in a plain envelope once a year. You can work out a code with your bank for it to be sure that, when someone claiming to be you calls, the person on the other end of the telephone actually is you. Most common is to give your mother's maiden name. The supercautious will use another code because that is both too traditional and too easy for an outsider to obtain from public records.

The largest banks operate throughout the country. Private banks are concentrated in Geneva because most of their clients historically were French.

Many Swiss bankers (and even bank employees at the bottom of the totem pole, such as tellers and switchboard operators) speak English. They also speak German, French, and Italian as a matter of course and frequently speak other languages as well, such as Spanish.

STILL THE SAFEST WEALTH PROTECTION HAVEN

Based on liquidity ratio (a function of how easily a bank

can cover its outstanding obligations by selling off its assets), the following banks are the safest in Switzerland, and perhaps the world.

Any bank listed below will open accounts for new clients only if they are known to the bank or are recommended by an advisor or correspondent with whom the bank is familiar:

- Banque Financière de La Cité
- Banque Lausannoise de Portefeuilles
- BFZ Bankfinanz
- Dreyfus Söhne & Cie.
- Ferrier Lullin & Cie. SA
- FIBI Bank (Switzerland) Ltd.
- Guyerzeller Bank
- PBZ Privatbank Zürich
- Ruegg Bank Zürich

THE CANTON ALTERNATIVE

A little-known option, for small accounts in particular, is the banks run by the various cantons. These banks have no minimum deposits. Also, they are safer than the big national banks because each canton ensures deposits in its cantonal bank. They perform portfolio management in common to be able to compete with the nationwide Swiss banks. We have included a list for the major areas.

Swiss banks are extremely efficient and highly profitable for their shareholders. They also are pretty safe. The five largest Swiss banks have the highest equity-to-assets ratio of the large banks in any country in the world. That means that they have capital and disclosed reserves that amount to well over 5 percent of the total amount that they have lent (only one major U.S. international bank does).

In addition, Swiss banks generally have substantial hidden reserves that they do not report. And they have very few problem loans, not having been active in financing developing countries or Texas oil drilling or California real estate (to name some problem banking businesses).

POLITICAL THREAT

The main political threat to Swiss banking secrecy comes not from the United States but from within the country itself. The Socialists frequently make political hay with the country's reputation as a haven for the ill-gotten gains of the world. Recently, a proposal by the Socialists that bank secrecy laws dating back to 1934 be lifted if banks knowingly accept flight capital was soundly defeated in a national referendum. But the issue will not go away. Under the Confederation's highly democratic form of government, a citizen's initiative to put the issue back on the ballot is always possible, although most Swiss do not believe this is a realistic threat.

Internationally, the Swiss mount a vigorous defense against their critics. Switzerland opposed attempts by the 24-nation Organization for Economic Cooperation and Development (OECD) to crack down on tax avoidance. It was backed in this effort by Luxembourg, Austria, and Portugal—which has hopes for Macau and the Atlantic island chains of the Azores and Madeira.

Needless to say, the United States is a strong supporter of this OECD move. Not being inside the European Community, the Swiss are relatively immune to pressures from their European neighbors to stop acting as a haven.

U.S. BANKS IN SWITZERLAND

Many U.S. banks operate in Switzerland, but most of them shun individual (as opposed to corporate) customers. One that remained in the business of serving high-net-worth private banking customers, American Express International Bank, which controlled Switzerland's Trade Development Bank (TDB), finally found the contradiction between Swiss banking secrecy and American extraterritorial reach to be too much. It sold TDB to Compagnie de Banque et d'Investissement, a Geneva-based private bank, and which then bought Cambio Valorenbank in 1993.

American banks such as Bankers Trust and Citicorp are also major players in private banking in Switzerland. They are not private in the sense of protecting the identities of clients from the United States; clients must sign a waiver of bank secrecy if their home country requires information on their Swiss bank accounts. That is one reason not to have a private bank account with an American bank in Switzerland if you are American.

There are ample choices, however. There are about 140 foreign banks licensed to operate in Switzerland. Furthermore, there are more than 100 finance companies of foreign ownership. They account for 15 percent and 23 percent, respectively, of Swiss banking assets and earnings.

COMPETITION AND BANKING SECRECY

The arrival of new foreign banks increases competition in Swiss banking. In theory this is of interest to private banking customers, but in practice the rise of competition threatens banking secrecy. Unlike the partnerships, these banks have branches and subsidiaries in the United States that can be held hostage to force them to disgorge information on clients' accounts abroad in cases where clients are accused of tax evasion, insider trading, money laundering, or other offenses against American law.

A new bank operation was recently opened in Switzerland by Finansbank AS, which is a Turkish banking and insurance company listed on the Istanbul stock exchange. FB (Suisse) is located in Geneva.

Baring Brothers, the British bank, which had been operating as a joint venture with Banque Lombard Odier, opted to set up its own bank for private individuals. National Westminster, the British bank, took control of its former joint venture bank with Nestlé, called Handelsbank. Barclays has opened up Barclays International private banking offices in Zurich, Geneva, and Lugano.

After Bank Leu was discredited as a private banking specialist, the sixth largest bank in Switzerland ultimately lost so much business that in 1990 it fell prey to a hostile takeover—itself a rarity in Switzerland—mounted by Crédit Suisse. To reduce pressure from the American authorities, the New York branch was reduced to a representation office and laid off much of the staff. The effect of the bank's involvement in the Dennis Levine and Guinness Distillers insider trading cases in the United States and Britain—and its inability to stop details from being revealed to investigators—seems to have doomed Bank Leu.

The fate of Leu is believed by some to herald consolidation among Swiss private banks. This, however is not the general consensus. All banks were required to meet new internationally agreed ratios of equity to assets (the same ratios that are causing havoc among solvent U.S. thrifts) by 1992, but the Swiss banks had already met the standards. In other European centers, such as Paris and Cologne, formerly private banks have had to open their capital to public shareholders to meet the ratios, ending traditions of partnership structure often several hundred years old.

PROFITABILITY

The profitability of Swiss banks is hard to determine, in part because some banks report no information on this matter, being private in ownership. However, a recent study by Dr. Kurt Hauri, chairman of the Swiss Banking Commission, showed that, after the 1987 stock market crash, when 330 banks had a fall in operating results, only 86 reported lower earnings.

Even more astonishingly, 46 banks that had operating losses related to the crash nonetheless reported a rise in profits. This was done by drawing on hidden reserves. Their Federal Banking Commission allowed Swiss banks to report as profits money extracted from their hidden reserves.

Now, however, the Swiss Federal Banking Commission requires that all allocations from hidden reserves to offset losses be reported. Furthermore, any allocation to profits amounting to more than 3 percent of capital or 30 percent of net earnings must be reported.

These thresholds are still quite high but will nonetheless force banks to report more honestly. And the ability of undercapitalized private banks to cover up losses will be hampered.

THE DUTCH CONNECTION

One way to invest in a broad portfolio with a Swiss bank without too much money is through the Dutch mutual fund group Robeco (Rotterdamse Belegings Co.). The Dutch group was founded in 1929. The SEC doesn't approve of it because it is publicly listed and open ended. (In the United States, publicly listed mutual funds are closed ended.)

In practice, this means that Robeco intervenes in the Dutch stock market to repurchase its shares or sell them to keep the price close to net-asset value. Legally, the funds in the group are incorporated investment institutions with variable capital.

The Robeco group is the largest mutual fund management group in the world outside the United States and Britain, with funds under management topping $15 billion. It offers four funds: Robeco, an equity fund aiming at worldwide blue chips; Rolinco, an equity fund aiming at growth—but still prudent; Rodamco, a diversified international real estate investment company (whose largest investments are in the United States) aiming at appreciation and income; and Rorento, a bond fund, a fixed-interest accumulator trust aiming at earning interest and capital gains. Investors can switch among the funds without fees. The Dutch fund management group has opened a bank in Geneva, Banque Robeco (Suisse), and which acts as a distribution center for Robeco products outside the Netherlands.

A few years ago, the Dutch government began to fuss about nondistributed earnings being reinvested in the funds and threatened to make trouble about getting identification from new clients (as part of a crackdown on tax evasion within the Netherlands). To help circumvent these developments the group opened its bank in Geneva. The whole operation still is essentially run out of Rotterdam, with the added advantage of Swiss secrecy and multicurrency efficiency.

Deposits or withdrawals can be made in any major currency. The highly efficient computerized system automatically reinvests all dividends (without withholding taxes, as would be required were Robeco Swiss rather than Dutch). The minimum investment is $5,000, and you can divide it among as many as four funds to best match your investment needs.

These folks speak English well: Robeco N.V., Heer Kobelweg 133, Postbus 973, NL-3000 Rotterdam, the Netherlands; tel. (31-10) 465-0711; fax (31-10) 465-1544.

INSURANCE ANNUITIES

Swiss annuities minimize the risk posed by U.S. annuities. They are heavily regulated, unlike in the United States, to avoid any potential funding problem. They denominate accounts in the strong Swiss franc, compared to the weakening dollar. And the annuity payout is guaranteed.

Swiss annuities are exempt from the 35-percent withholding tax imposed by Switzerland on bank account interest received by foreigners. Annuities do not have to be reported to Swiss or U.S. tax authorities. They are not a foreign financial account for the purpose of U.S. reporting requirements.

A U.S. purchaser of an annuity is required to pay a 1-percent U.S. federal excise tax on the purchase of any policy from a foreign company. This is much like the sales tax rule that says that if a person shops in a different state, with a lower sales tax than his home state, when he gets home he is required to mail a check to his home state's sales tax department for the difference in sales tax rates.

The federal excise tax form (IRS form 720) does not ask for details of the policy bought or from whom it was bought—it merely asks for a calculation of 1 percent tax of any foreign policies purchased. This is a one-time tax at the time of purchase; it is not an ongoing tax. It is the responsibility of the U.S. taxpayer to report the Swiss annuity or other foreign insurance policy. Swiss insurance companies do not report anything to any government agency, Swiss or U.S.—not the initial purchase of the policy, nor the payments into it, nor interest and dividends earned.

Earnings on annuities during the deferral period are not taxable in the United States until income is paid, or when they are liquidated, following exactly the same tax rules as for annuities issued by U.S. insurance companies.

Swiss annuities can be placed in a U.S. tax-sheltered pension plans, such as IRA, Keogh, or corporate plans, or such a plan can be rolled over into a Swiss annuity. (To put a Swiss annuity in a U.S. pension plan, all that is required is a U.S. trustee, such as a bank or other institution, and that the annuity contract be held in the United States by that trustee. Many banks offer "self-directed" pension plans for a very small annual administration fee, and these plans can easily be used for this purpose.)

Investment in Swiss annuities is on a "no-load" basis, front end or back end. The investments can be canceled at any time, without a loss of principal, and with all principal, interest, and dividends payable if canceled after one year. (If canceled in the first year, there is a small penalty of about SFr 500, plus loss of interest.)

A fairly new Swiss annuity product, Swiss Plus (first offered in 1991), brings together the benefits of Swiss bank accounts and Swiss deferred annuities, without the drawbacks—presenting the best Swiss investment advantages for American investors.

Swiss Plus is a convertible annuity account, offered only by Elvia Life of Geneva. Elvia Life is a $2 billion-strong company, serving 220,000 clients, of which 57 percent are living in Switzerland and 43 percent abroad. The account can be denominated in the Swiss franc, the U.S. dollar, the German mark, or the European Currency Unit (ECU), and the investor can switch at any time from one to another. Or an investor can diversify the account by investing in more than one currency, and still change the currency at any time during the accumulation period—up until beginning to receive income or withdrawing the capital.

The ECU currency was created in 1979. It is composed of a currency basket of 11 European currencies, and its value is calculated daily by the European Commission according to the changes in value of the underlying currencies. The ECU is composed of a weighted mean of all member currencies of the European Monetary System. Since the ECU changes its balance to reflect changes in exchange rates and interest rates between these currencies, the ECU tends to limit exchange rate risk and interest rate risks.

Although called an annuity, Swiss Plus acts more like a savings account than a deferred annuity. But it is operated under an insurance company's umbrella, so that it conforms to the IRS' definition of an annuity and, as such, compounds tax-free until it is liquidated or converted into an income annuity later on.

Swiss Plus accounts earn approximately the same return as long-term government bonds in the same currency in which the account is denominated (European Community bonds in the case of the ECU), less a half-percent management fee.

Interest and dividend income are guaranteed by a Swiss insurance company. Swiss government regulations protect investors against either underperformance or overcharging.

Swiss Plus offers instant liquidity, a rarity in annuities. All capital, plus all accumulated interest and dividends, can be freely accessible after the first year. During the first year 100 percent of the principal is freely accessible, less a SFr 500 fee, and loss of the interest. So if all funds are needed quickly, either for an emergency or for another investment, there is no lock-in period as there is with most U.S. annuities.

Upon maturity of the account, the investor can choose between a lump sum payout (paying capital gains tax on accumulated earnings only), rolling the funds into an income annuity (paying capital gains taxes only as future income payments are received, and then only on the portion representing accumulated earnings), or extend the scheduled term by giving notice in advance of the originally scheduled date (and continue to defer tax on accumulated earnings).

According to Swiss law, insurance policies—including annuity contracts—cannot be seized by creditors. They also cannot be included in a Swiss bankruptcy procedure. Even if a U.S. court expressly orders the seizure of a Swiss annuity account or its inclusion in a bankruptcy estate, the account will not be seized by Swiss authorities, provided that it has been structured the right way.

There are two requirements. First, a U.S. resident who buys a life insurance policy from a Swiss insurance company must designate his or her spouse or descendants, or a third party (if done so irrevocably) as beneficiaries. Second, to avoid suspicion of making a fraudulent conveyance to avoid a specific judgment, under Swiss law the person must have purchased the policy or designated the beneficiaries not less than six months before any bankruptcy decree or collection process.

The policyholder can also protect the policy by converting a designation of spouse or children into an irrevocable designation when he becomes aware of the fact that his creditors will seize his assets and that a court might compel him to repatriate the funds in the insurance policy. If he is subsequently ordered to revoke the designation of the beneficiary and to liquidate the policy he will not be able to do so as the insurance company will not accept his instructions because of the irrevocable designation of the beneficiaries.

Article 81 of the Swiss insurance law provides that if a policyholder has made a revocable designation of spouse or children as beneficiaries, they automatically become policyholders and acquire all rights if the policyholder is declared bankrupt. In such a case, the original policyholder therefore automatically loses control over the policy and also his right to demand the liquidation of the policy and the repatriation of funds. A court therefore cannot compel the policyholder to liquidate the policy or otherwise repatriate his funds. If the spouse or children notify the insurance company of the bankruptcy, the insurance company will note that in its records. Even if the original policyholder sends instructions because a court has ordered him to do so, the insurance company will ignore those instructions. It is important that the company be notified promptly of the bankruptcy, so that it does not inadvertently follow the original policyholder's instructions because it wasn't told of the bankruptcy.

If the policyholder has designated his spouse or his children as beneficiaries of the insurance policy, the insurance policy is protected from his creditors regardless of whether the designation is revocable or irrevocable. The policyholder may therefore designate his spouse or children as beneficiaries on a revocable basis and revoke this designation before the policy expires, if at such time there is no threat from any creditors.

These laws are part of fundamental Swiss law. They were not created to make Switzerland an asset-protection haven. In the Swiss annuity situation, the insurance policy is not being protected by the Swiss courts and government because of any especial concern for the American investor, but because the principle of protection of insurance policies is a fundamental part of Swiss law—for the protection of the Swiss themselves. Insurance is for the family, not something to be taken by creditors or other claimants. No Swiss lawyer would even waste his time bringing such a case.

CONTACT INFORMATION

The only way for North Americans to get information on Swiss annuities is to send a letter to a Swiss insurance broker. This is because very few transactions can be concluded

Switzerland

directly with foreigners either with a Swiss insurance company or with regular Swiss insurance agents.

When you contact a Swiss insurance broker, be sure to include (in addition to your name, address, and telephone number) your date of birth, marital status, citizenship, number of children and their ages, name of spouse, and a clear definition of your financial objectives (possibly on what dollar amount you would like to invest).

Only one firm specializes in dealing with English-speaking investors, and everybody in the firm speaks excellent English. They are also familiar with U.S. laws affecting the purchase of Swiss annuities. Contact Mr. Jürg Lattmann. JML Swiss Investment Counsellors AG, Dept. 212, Germaniastrasse 55, 8033 Zurich, Switzerland; tel. (41-1) 363-2510, fax (41-1) 361-4074, attn. Dept. 212.

SWISS BANKS

Bank Julius Baer, Bahnhofstrasse 36, CH-8021; tel. (41-1) 228-7111; fax (41-1) 211-2560
Bank Leu, Bahnhofstrasse 32, CH-8001 Zurich; tel. (41-1) 219-1111; fax (41-1) 219-3197
Banque Union de Crédit, Rue de Mont Blanc 3, P.O. Box 1816, CH-1211 Geneva 1; tel. (41-22) 732-7939; fax (41-22) 732-5089
Crédit Suisse, Paradeplatz 8, CH-8021 Zurich; tel. (41-1) 333-1111; fax (41-1) 332-5555
Swiss Bank Corp., Aeschenvorstadt, CH-4002 Basel; tel. (41-61) 202020; fax (41-61) 204576
Union Bank of Switzerland, Bahnhofstrasse 45, CH-8021 Zurich; tel. (41-1) 234-1111; fax (41-1) 234-6480

CHAPTER 12

LIECHTENSTEIN

People tend to think of Liechtenstein, if they think of Liechtenstein at all, as the Postage Stamp Principality. The country's major export earner used to be postage stamps, prized by collectors. However, this has not been the case since the 1950s. Since that time, this tiny Rhine Valley principality has become an export-oriented industrial state and banking center.

Liechtenstein is a tiny country, measuring only 16 miles long by 3.5 miles wide, sandwiched between Switzerland and Austria, and has a population of 28,000. As much as 52 percent of the working population is in manufacturing; 45 percent in service industries, such as tourism, hotels, restaurants, and banking; and 3 percent in agriculture. Like Switzerland, Liechtenstein is on Europe's top shelf in terms of per capita income. Government is by constitutional monarchy, with the Prince of Liechtenstein as the head of state. His power extends to sanctioning laws and, in an emergency, decreeing law. The people of Liechtenstein participate in government through the election of the legislative body and through direct referendum. The legislature is responsible for legislation, drawing up treaties, approving taxes, and supervising the affairs of government. It frequently submits legislation directly to the citizens by referendum.

The major industrial activities involve the manufacture of machinery and precision instruments, textiles, and chemical and pharmaceutical products. Two of the largest Liechtenstein-owned companies are Hilti and Ivoclar. Hilti, which manufactures construction fastenings, has offices throughout the world. Ivoclar manufactures dental products and is the world's second-largest producer of false teeth.

Another important component of Liechtenstein's economy is its banking industry; the country is a prime location for trusts, investment companies, and holding companies. The country has three banks: Bank in Liechtenstein, which is owned by the Prince of Liechtenstein Foundation and controlled by the prince; Liechtenstein Landesbank, which is owned by the government; the Vervaltung-und Privatbank, a privately owned bank. Foreign-owned banks and trust companies are not permitted. Government regulators stress local accountability of management, and professional qualifications are required for all company managers. One cannot just open up a package company service and offer Liechtenstein corporations, trusts, or foundations.

Like Liechtenstein itself, the three banks are very small, but they are growing fast. Balance sheets for the three totaled SFr 4.4 billion in 1980, but this figure rose to SFr 18.9 billion in 1991. Both the Bank in Liechtenstein and the Liechtenstein Landesbank currently have assets of SFr 7.6 billion, whereas the Vervaltung-und-Privatbank has SFr 4.4 billion.

Liechtenstein is not a financial center in its own right, but it is an important regional banking hub within the Swiss financial center. The three banks and the employment-market conditions are not sufficient to support a stock exchange in Liechtenstein or to maintain a capital and money market there. The three banks benefit hugely, however, by their access to Switzerland's international banking system, currency, and capital markets. At the same time, Switzerland gains much from Liechtenstein. The three banks effect a lot of investments in or through Swiss banks. Many Liechtenstein holding companies maintain accounts in Swiss banks. As a result, these holding companies provide an important foundation to the Swiss banking system. The primary use of Liechtenstein is not as a banking center, but as a tax haven base for holding companies, private foundations, and family foundations. The banks, and a host of specialized trust companies, provide management services for these entities.

Liechtenstein is politically and economically stable and enjoys favorable tax legislation, including the holding-company privilege. The economy is integrated with Switzerland's, and the Swiss franc is the legal tender. The country's workers maintain a high productivity rate, and the banks and trust companies provide a broad range of services for both regional and international clients. Its central location in Europe allows easy access from other European countries, and there is only a six-hour time difference between Liechtenstein and the East Coast of the United States.

The Banking Act of 1960 basically follows the Swiss banking law but is generally stricter, as in the granting of bank licenses. Most users consider Liechtenstein to be more secretive than Switzerland. In a legal sense, as well as a subjective one, this is certainly true because Liechtenstein does not have any double taxation or exchange of information treaties (except for a minor double tax treaty with Austria, primarily to cover the number of people who work across the border).

Liechtenstein has often come under fire as a result of its liberal taxation and banking secrecy. It has been accused of harboring "flight capital," money that is taken out of a country in order to get it beyond the reach of local tax authorities. Liechtenstein holds that in the case of EC nations, where there are no restrictions on the transfer of capital, no flight capital can exist. The banks will not accept money from any country where there are specific laws against the exportation of capital.

Switzerland has been pressuring Liechtenstein to conform to its regulations on money laundering, but Liechtenstein has been resisting this pressure because it has had its own strict laws against this in place for decades. Liechtenstein's banks will not accept any money from illegal activities as far as they are recognizable. In 1989, the country stopped accepting foreign funds from offshore firms unless they were represented by an attorney registered in Liechtenstein. Even Swiss lawyers are not acceptable.

SECRECY GUARANTEED BY LAW

Liechtenstein's banking system is more secure than Switzerland's. Even though the banks are required to keep records of their clients' identities, they may not make them public. This extends to trustees and accountants—to anyone, in fact, who has a connection with the banking industry. These people are subject to the disciplinary powers of Liechtenstein's Upper Court. There have been no violations to date. Because it is a very small and socially close-knit country, there are not the masses of underpaid bank clerks ready to be bribed, as occurs all too often in impoverished Caribbean tax havens.

It takes an order from a Liechtenstein court to release the bank record of an account holder. Since there is no mutual legal-assistance treaty, such a court case is a major undertaking because Liechtenstein has no obligation to honor a foreign request. A foreign government might succeed in case of definite proof of a violation of Liechtenstein law—such as clear evidence that the proceeds of an armored car robbery went directly to a specific Liechtenstein account.

The secrecy of information disclosed to Liechtenstein authorities, tax and otherwise, is guaranteed by law. Liechtenstein law prohibits a court from providing assistance to foreign authorities in cases involving political, taxation, and exchange-control matters.

Switzerland, on the other hand, has a treaty obligation to release information at the behest of a foreign court order with regard to something that is also a crime in Switzerland, although the request must still go through a Swiss court (see the chapter on Switzerland for more detail).

Liechtenstein has U.S.-style trust laws. This could be useful in creating an obstacle to the taxmen. A trust could be used to protect someone on assignment in a country that likes to tax worldwide assets, such as the United States. It could also protect a foreign spouse of an American, safeguarding his or her assets from the IRS in the event of the American's death.

Liechtenstein does not have the 35-percent withholding tax that Switzerland does. Because there is very little investment in Liechtenstein itself, the investments are subject to the withholding taxes of those countries where the money is invested. If, for example, a Liechtenstein account or trust invests in the United States, it is subject to a 30-percent withholding tax. Because there are no double-taxation agreements, you would not be able to get this money back, even if you reported it to the IRS. The advantage to this is that no tax information is exchanged with another country's government. Normally, a Liechtenstein-based entity would simply invest in offshore mutual funds and bank deposits in countries without a withholding tax.

Banks in Liechtenstein have no official minimum deposit requirements, but the goal is to lure high-net-worth individuals. You will not be able to get discretionary portfolio management for under SFr 1 million. Trusts and limited companies must pay an annual local tax of either 0.1 percent of the capital or SFr 1,000, whichever is higher. The banks also charge a management fee of 0.5 percent of assets per year. Because of this, you should have enough money in the country to make it worth your while.

For anyone considering opening an account with a Swiss or Austrian bank, Liechtenstein is worth a look. It has all the benefits of the other two—a stable, growing economy, rock-solid currency, political stability, and ease of access—plus a few of its own. The county's secrecy laws make it a much tougher nut to crack than Switzerland, and, unlike Austria, it has no double-taxation agreements (except with Austria itself).

ANSTALTS

Liechtenstein is perhaps best known for the *anstalt* (sometimes called "the establishment" in English), an entity unique to Liechtenstein law, which is something of a hybrid between a trust and a corporation. Its charter can be written very flexibly and, depending on the desired result, take on more trust or corporation characteristics. Really sophisticated investors with good tax lawyers have had these tailored to meet specific criteria and then obtained IRS private-letter rulings recognizing the *anstalt* as either a trust or corporation, as desired.

The regulation of anstalts, foundations, companies, and trusts in Liechtenstein is extremely strict, but primarily through regulating the managers, not through prying into the internal affairs of the entity or its holdings. The quality of management services available in Liechtenstein is superb.

Creating a family foundation can sometimes be more useful than a trust, since it falls outside of trust rules, and a foundation does not have an owner. This is an extremely complex subject, and top-quality tax advice is needed. We are only mentioning that it is a possibility for those in a position to use it properly.

Only very limited information about the persons involved in individual companies is available to the public. The beneficial owners of a company do not appear by name in any register, and their identities are not even disclosed to the Liechtenstein authorities. On the other hand, the members of the board of directors are exposed to publicity, and any member of the public can discover their identities by searching the Commercial Register. At least one member of the board must be resident in Liechtenstein and must possess certain professional qualifications.

The trust law of Liechtenstein is itself not only of great practical interest, but also of theoretical interest. This is because Liechtenstein is one of the few countries with a civil-law tradition, but which has made the attempt of incorporating into its law the concept of the common-law trust. The Liechtenstein legislature of 1926 laid great stress on achieving a faithful reproduction of the English, and partly the U.S., system of trust law. The Liechtenstein law specifically permits a trust to have a clause allowing itself to be governed by the rules of law of any common-law country. Thus the Liechtenstein courts would be obliged to apply the specified law (such as English, Bermuda, or Delaware) to interpreting any controversy regarding the trust instrument.

The trust instrument must be deposited with the Commercial Registry but is not subject to public examination. (A trust has the option of requesting full commercial registration, in which case the document is open to inspection.)

A Liechtenstein trust is frequently used to control a family fortune, with the trust assets being shares in holding companies controlling the relevant businesses.

LIECHTENSTEIN BANKS

- Bank in Liechtenstein, Vaduz; tel. (41-75) 51122; fax (41-75) 51522; contact Réné Ott.
- Liechtensteinische Landesbank, Vaduz; tel. (41-75)68811; fax (41-75)68358
- Verwaltungs-und-Privatbank, Postfach 885, FL-9490 Vaduz; tel. (41-75)56655; fax: (41-75) 56500; contact Markus Meier.

CHAPTER 13
LUXEMBOURG

By tradition, the Grand Duchy of Luxembourg has served as a center of tax evasion for clients from neighboring Belgium. Since 1970, it has also become a major center for German banks that use it to provide loans to corporate customers not subject to reserve requirements and to deal in gold without the value-added tax. There are now more than 150 banks in Luxembourg.

It is fear of the attractions of Switzerland and Austria, which are not in the European Community, that has motivated Luxembourg to defend bank secrecy and clients' rights to be exempt from withholding taxes from pressures from its larger neighbors in the EC. About a quarter of the population is employed directly or indirectly by the offshore banking sector. As much as 42 percent of the county's business comes from private banking.

The authorities keep close watch over the solvency of banks operating in the country but are considerably more relaxed about whether banks' clients have paid taxes on the money they are depositing. Luxembourg, which is a member of the Common Market, spearheaded the resistance to a continent-wide withholding tax system, for example, that would have applied to many users of its banking system.

But on the other hand, former U.S. Attorney General

Richard Thornburgh complimented the Luxembourg authorities for their cooperation in the investigation of drug money. Similarly, late in the autumn of 1989, Luxembourg's prime minister, Jacques Santer, maneuvered to discuss with the Socialist president of neighboring France the question of whether Luxembourg bank secrecy laws should be changed. President Mitterrand ultimately signed an agreement that granted Luxembourg the right to keep accounts of banking clients secret unless criminal links could be established.

To prove its determination to resist mounting pressure from the EC, Luxembourg had as early as 1989 rushed through legislation enshrining banking secrecy as law. The measure was enacted as a decree and signed by Grand Duke Jean on March 24, thus avoiding any delay or debate. Before that, the government had obtained all-party support through the financial industry supervisory committee of the Luxembourg parliament and the approval of the Council of State, which advises on legislation.

Previously, banking secrecy had derived from a provision in the penal code referring to professional secrecy in general and penalties for violating it (the so-called midwives' law) and recent laws amending or clarifying its effect. This was felt to be insufficient at a time when it was being proposed to introduce a Continent-wide withholding tax (subsequently defeated) and mutual assistance and exchange of information between the tax authorities of the EC.

PRIVACY FOR MIDWIVES

The Luxembourg bank secrecy law of 1989 did not invent the concept of banking secrecy; it merely codified older rules. The real origin of the bank secrecy law, according to Banking Commissioner Pierre Jaans, is a nineteenth-century law that obliged bankers to observe the same respect for privacy as it applied to midwives. Midwives were forbidden to give out information that may have been revealed by the mothers while giving birth (about, for example, who the father might be).

The Luxembourg secrecy law is asymmetrical. A bank's assets (its loans) must be disclosed to the Banking Commission and to the home office. This enables strict controls to be maintained on the solidity and honesty of Luxembourg banks. For example, they are not permitted to lend to related companies the way Hong Kong banks have done. No secrecy operates on the loan side.

On the other hand, no information about deposits may be provided without violating the law, which, as in Switzerland, results in fines and imprisonment. (The prison term and the amount of the fines are almost identical to the Swiss penalties.) Under Luxembourg law, the depositor cannot decide to waive banking secrecy if he wants to (e.g., if he is being sued). Under Swiss law, if his arm is twisted by the home courts, a depositor has the right to ask the bank he deals with to lift secrecy.

Still untested in Luxembourg courts is the practice used by many foreign-branch U.S. banks with U.S. depositors—that of requiring a prior waiver of bank secrecy when one tries to open an account. Commissioner Jaans thinks that the waiver would have no force under Luxembourg law.

If the bank gave information to the American authorities without being authorized to do so by a Luxembourg court, the client still could sue the bank. And the bank still would be liable for violating the Luxembourg law on secrecy.

AN "OFFSHORE" MOUNTAINTOP

Luxembourg is newer to international banking than other mountaintop countries where the people speak German dialects and the banks observe laws on banking secrecy. Although the country's own banks were started in the nineteenth century by foreigners (who still own a part of the capital of every Luxembourg bank), the Grand Duchy became an offshore banking center only two decades ago. (It is an "offshore" center that is in the middle of Europe and is not an island.)

The development of international banking in Luxembourg was spawned by the same forces that fueled the growth of the Euromarkets in the mid-1960s: the U.S. interest equalization tax, which drove U.S. corporations to borrow abroad; restrictions on capital flows and lending ratios in Germany; withholding tax in Switzerland; exchange controls in neighboring countries, such as France; and new rules requiring reporting of bank accounts in nearby Holland.

About 40 percent of all Luxembourg banks' total assets and liabilities are in German marks, and another one-third are in U.S. dollars. This contrasts with Switzerland and the Channel Islands, where most business still is done in the home currency. Only 13 percent of the banking business of Luxembourg is in the currency of the country.

GROWTH FACTORS FOR LUXEMBOURG BANKS

The German decision to impose a 10 percent withholding tax on interest and dividends sent billions of deutschemarks over the border into Luxembourg in 1989. Because of the Swiss 35-percent withholding tax on foreign-owned bank accounts, stocks, and bonds, many Swiss banks have been brought into the Grand Duchy, following their customers who had moved their money out of Switzerland.

Also helping Luxembourg business has been the EC system for mutual recognition of supervised mutual funds, the UCITS directive. (UCITS are Undertakings for Collective Investment in Transferable Securities.) UCITS recognized in one EC jurisdiction may be marketed in all 12 countries. Beneficiaries include Luxembourg funds called SICAVs. (SICAV stands for Société d'Investissement Collective à Capital Variable.) The Luxembourg law on SICAVs was first passed in 1983. Among its other effects, it eliminated the stamp duty and introduced supervision of funds. Fund management is a Luxembourg growth industry. The number of funds is now more than 700.

VULNERABILITY TO INTERNATIONAL SHOCKS

The solvency of Luxembourg banks, however well protected, and the stability of the Belgian-Luxembourg franc, however great, are not the only things depositors need to worry about. Luxembourg is a booking and transaction center for the international currency and bond markets. This means that deposits in its banks depend on the security of the whole international banking system, in particular those of Germany and the United States. Most of the clients in Luxembourg are multinational corporations, not individuals. If you think the system is shaky and you worry about U.S. bank solvency, you are better off in Switzerland—particularly if you have sufficiently large sums so that the Swiss will not snub you. If you are reasonably confident that the U.S. banking system will survive or if you do not have $100,000 in loose cash to open your account, try Luxembourg. Your privacy will be better protected.

Unlike Switzerland, Liechtenstein, and Austria, Luxembourg is not neutral. Nor is it a republic. Luxembourg is a Grand Duchy with a hereditary ruler, Grand Duke Jean. Luxembourgers commonly speak three languages: French, German, and their own peculiar version of German called Letzebuergesch. Like some of the Swiss-German dialects, it is incomprehensible even if you have studied German for years. Being polyglots from early days makes the locals good at languages. English is widely spoken and commonly used by everyone in the banking business—from the doorman and the telephone operator on up.

Luxembourg is a member of NATO and of the European Community, is a part of the Benelux group of countries, and is in full monetary and economic union with its larger neighbor, Belgium.

BEARER SHARES

Luxembourg, like other Continental countries, uses bearer shares. Treasurers of Luxembourg companies or managers of local mutual funds really do not know who the owners are. As a result, it is impossible to prevent Americans from buying Luxembourg SICAV shares.

If you want to buy offshore a fund investing in U.S. Treasury bonds, not subject to withholding, you can do it in Luxembourg but probably nowhere else. To try to find the money to cover the huge U.S. government deficit, the Treasury has recently begun offering bonds without withholding to foreign investors and mutual funds.

The Swiss swore they would not sell them to Americans. The British swore they would not and used the corporate rolls of their mutual funds to make sure that they did not. The Luxembourg SICAVs seem to have slipped through the regulatory net.

Luxembourg got into the banking business because it had an old, attractive law on holding companies. A holding company under local law is not taxed on dividends, income, capital gain, or any surpluses when it winds up. This law led to the creation of the first investment funds in Luxembourg—the key to the local development of private banking. Initially, they were holding companies. A 1983 law now allows investment fund companies, or SICAVs.

SICAVs are regulated by the Monetary Institute, which supervises their prospectuses and publicity. There must be an annual outside audit. They are subject to fees and taxes when being set up and an annual fee of 0.06 percent of assets. Luxembourg investment companies must be separately incorporated (so there is no easy switching between funds with different goals in the same group as in Britain or the offshore British islands). They are closed-end funds that are traded publicly but are redeemed at net asset value—the way open-ended funds are in the United States.

Your Luxembourg bank will aim to enroll you in its SICAVs unless you have a great sum of money to invest. The banks earn fees for managing your money that run from 1.5 percent to 3 percent a year. And they earn other commissions when they buy and sell bonds or stocks in the fund. Remember to get the share certificate if you don't want to have to declare your account to the U.S. Treasury.

The Luxembourg government gets its slice, too—in fees and taxes on the funds and in taxing the large number of people needed by the funds for administration. This enables the applied rate of corporate taxes that banks must pay to be kept low.

READY-TO-WEAR BANKING

Luxembourg is the center of ready-to-wear private banking. You and your banker (who legally acts as broker and mutual fund salesman) pick a group of SICAV funds to meet your investment objectives. SICAVs accept modest payments. The total you invest through Luxembourg need not exceed $25,000, the minimum at most local banks.

The SICAVs are closely regulated by the Banking Commission as to how they invest and how they advertise. They are seeking the right to advertise in foreign newspapers and bring in more business, something Luxembourg is negotiating with the EC. Of course, the country will not dismantle bank secrecy to be allowed to peddle mutual funds.

Luxembourg has advantages and disadvantages in the private international-bank-haven sweepstakes. For Europeans, this is a convenient place in which to bank. The proverbial Euromarket investor is supposed to be a Belgian dentist, who needs only to drive over the nearby border to open his account and doesn't even need to change his money. The Luxembourgers treat Belgian currency as legal tender.

For Americans, this tiny country lacks such attractions as the ski slopes of Switzerland, the Seven-Mile Beach of Grand Cayman, and the Gulf Stream of the Channel Islands. Luxembourg's tax system is not very favorable to residents, so don't move here. (Luxembourg taxes are negotiable, but only if you are a big German bank.)

Luxembourg does have advantages over other offshore

sites, however. As noted, there is no 35 percent withholding tax on interest and dividends, as in Switzerland. Payout of dividends, bond interest, and bank interest is gross of any Luxembourg taxation, with no withholding at the source, no 1099s, and no listing of your Social Security number.

Because Luxembourg has very few double-taxation treaties compared to Switzerland, however, it is a bad place to use as a haven for collecting funds from other countries with high withholding taxes because you will not be able to offset these taxes against taxes you otherwise would owe at home. Once the withholding tax has been paid on funds transiting through Luxembourg, it is mostly lost. Luxembourg does have double-taxation treaties with some countries, but all those treaties specifically exempt Luxembourg holding companies.

MIR WOLLE BLEIWE WAT MIR SIN

That subhead is a bit of Letzebuergesch. It means, "We want to remain as we are." It is the unofficial slogan of Luxembourg, part of the refrain of a nineteenth-century song.

Switzerland has been the target of U.S., French, and Italian demands that it help catch tax evaders and turn away flight capital, but foreign tax authorities have a hard time putting pressure on Luxembourg. Even Socialists inside the country support bank secrecy.

Little Luxembourg has three parties, all of which are in favor of banks (which employ 17 percent of the local population and contribute even more to the gross national product). Its banks are not world-scale enterprises that need to have a branch in Los Angeles and a subsidiary in New York. As a result, Luxembourg is almost immune to the kind of pressure brought to bear against Switzerland.

Another advantage over Switzerland is that subscription and stamp taxes (transaction taxes) are either lower or nonexistent. No stamp tax is payable on securities or bond purchases. Nor is there a turnover tax (value-added tax) on gold purchases.

LOOMING EC LIBERALIZATION

There is a threat to this tiny, peaceable bank haven—the EC. In 1992, all internal barriers to the free flow of funds in the 12 European Common Market countries fell. This means that exchange-control obstacles to the movement of funds into Luxembourg from other European countries are due to end. Foreign banks and brokers will be free to move to Luxembourg to get more of this business—as long as they satisfy the country's strict Banking Commission of their soundness and solvency.

In this free-for-all, its fellow Europeans are not likely to want to let Luxembourg get all the business. They have two options. They can either pass bank secrecy laws of their own to offer comparable terms in their own banking systems or they can put pressure on little Luxembourg to dismantle its system. Chances are they will use the latter tactic.

Luxembourg has a lot of experience in dealing with foreign authorities. As a founding member of the 24-country Organization for Economic Cooperation and Development, Luxembourg tends to behave in a friendly and neighborly way to win friends and influence people. It uses the same sort of diplomacy in the 21-member Parliamentary Assembly of the Council of Europe, another international organization to which it belongs. In 1977 and 1978, these two international organizations decided to work together through the OECD Committee on Fiscal Affairs (CFA), a group of international civil servants, to improve tax collection.

In 1986, the OECD CFA produced a set of recommendations for curbing tax evasion that called for getting rid of "unduly restrictive bank secrecy." By OECD rules, recommendations can only advance out of committee if they are unanimously approved by all OECD countries.

Guess which OECD member country led the fight against the CFA recommendations? Luxembourg took the lead and was eventually joined by Austria, Switzerland, and Portugal. As a result, the CFA could make not recommendations but only "suggestions." These are not binding on member countries.

LUXEMBOURG BANKS

• Banque Générale de Luxembourg, 14 Rue Aldingen; tel. (352)45901
• Kredietbank S.A., 43 Blvd. Royal; tel. (352)47971; fax (352) 28267

CHAPTER 14

AUSTRIA

*G**lasnost* and *perestroika* are rewriting the political map of Europe—and changing the world of private banking. Democracy in Eastern Europe threatens private banking most in Austria.

It had long been rumored around the banking district of Vienna that Austria's strong bank secrecy laws enjoyed strong support from the U.S. government. The reason—Austrian banks had funneled regular payments to Soviet and East Bloc officials from the CIA. If Austrian bank secrecy had been lifted, these people would have faced not merely a bill for back taxes but a firing squad.

Now that the countries neighboring Austria (as well as others farther east with which Austria has traditionally maintained business relations) have moved away from Cold War confrontation, the U.S. government is pressuring the Austrians to amend their bank secrecy act to make it easier to lift. Under pressure from the United States, the European Community (which Austria wants to join), and the United Nations, which produced for ratification a convention on "due diligence" by countries to prevent illegal money movements in connection with drug dealing, Austria is committed to revising its banking regulations.

The present banking secrecy law requires that banks not

"disclose or make use of secrets which had been entrusted or made accessible to them solely due to the business relationships with customers." It is lifted in "criminal court proceedings" that include "intentional fiscal violations with the exception of fiscal petty offenses." It also does not apply "if the customer expressly and in writing consents to the disclosure of the secret."

Customers from foreign countries with which Austria is anxious to improve relations—notably the countries of the European Community—are liable to be asked expressly and in writing to allow their secrets to be disclosed. In addition, U.S. banks operating in Austria will usually require that customers from the United States sign such a waiver.

INTERNATIONAL PRESSURE

Helping put pressure on the Austrians is the increasing internationalization of their private banks, which until a few years ago were discreet and little known outside the country. The first break came when the 1987 reform of the banking law put all Austrian banks on a more equal footing, thereby encouraging the private banks to show that there were kinds of business they could do better for rich clients and corporations than could the largely state-controlled commercial banks. One private bank, Winter & Company, even decided to start advertising, although most private banks rely on word-of-mouth referral business.

Although some small banks had international links (FocoBank was formerly owned by the U.S. insurance group A.I.G. and now belongs to Royal Trust of Canada and specializes in private banking for North American clients, for example), a major break with the past came when Antoni Hacker, a private bank, was purchased by the powerful Deutsche Bank.

Austria plans to revise its banking secrecy act to bring it into line with revisions in other EC countries, as part of the application process. The EC is working on regulations to stop money laundering, expected to compromise between the commitment of the EC banks to "due diligence" and the general political trend toward deregulation.

It is not clear how far the Austrians will let themselves be pushed, and there are several bits of interesting fallout from Austrian banks as a result. First of all, many details of the U.S. Drug Enforcement Agency's attack on Manuel Noriega are being released by the Austrian banks—particularly the ones that make the U.S. agency look foolish. Also, Hungary's banks, which work more closely with Austrian banks than with those of any other Western country, are beginning to offer secret bank accounts. This means that they may pick up some business from their neighbor. The existence of a new, nearby banking secrecy haven strengthens the hands of Austrian bankers who want to resist giving in to the pressure from the United States and the EC to make it easier to lift banking secrecy.

One factor that helps Austria resist pressure to cut the privacy of its banks is the country's insularity. It is not the domicile of mutual funds that want to sell management services around Europe (as is Luxembourg). And Austria is not a major player in currency flows and insider trading. You cannot imagine people worrying about the "gnomes of Vienna" as former British Prime Minister Harold Wilson worried about the "gnomes of Zurich" when the pound was being clobbered.

UNEMBARRASSED BY NOTORIOUS DEPOSITORS

Austria is not headquarters to any world financial institutions like the Bank for International Settlements in Basel, Switzerland. As a result, Austrians are less likely than the Swiss to be embarrassed by either the antics of banks or the notoriety of their customers. In Austria, everything is much more low-key. Austrian Socialists do not make hay about banking secrecy laws the way Swiss ones do. In fact, the Austrian Socialists were part of the coalition that produced the laws in the first place.

Furthermore, Austria's provincial bankers are not as prone to international expansion as Swiss banks. There's no need to be. In contrast to the situation in Luxembourg, for example, Austrian banks face very little outside competition in the home market from foreign ones. (There are only a few foreign-owned banks offering private banking services in Austria that can act in a Trojan horse capacity in any outside effort to chip away at bank secrecy protection.) All these factors ensure that Austrian banks are more likely to be left alone to operate in secrecy than are banks from almost any other country.

IT HELPS TO SPEAK GERMAN

Provincialism has its negative side, too. The major problem with banking in Austria is that it may be difficult if you don't speak German. However, with patience and good will on your side—Austrians show patience and good will as a matter of course—you can find a bank officer who does speak your language.

Most middle- and top-level managers have studied English and understand it, but you cannot just assume that the clerks, tellers, doormen, and switchboard operators can speak English—as you can in almost any other banking center.

Another drawback to opening and dealing with an account in an Austrian bank is that there are no local branches. You can, however, combine banking with a visit to the Salzburg music festival, a comparative tasting of *sachertorte* in Vienna, or a trip down one of the ski runs at Innsbruck.

Austrian bank secrecy was two centuries old when it was codified into law in 1979. Under the law, it is a prisonable offense to reveal information about client bank accounts unless directed to do so by an Austrian court. The penalty is a jail term of as much as one year.

An Austrian court will direct banks to lift secrecy only on nonpetty criminal proceedings. Evasion of other than Austrian ones is a petty criminal act as defined by the law.

Moreover, it is specifically excluded from being grounds for lifting bank secrecy. Although Switzerland and other European countries are preparing legislation against insider trading, Austria has no such plans.

The Austrian schilling, like the Swiss franc, is a strong currency that moves closely with the German deutschemark. The Austrian central bank, the headquarters of which uncannily resemble the Federal Reserve building in Washington, D.C., helps to keep the parity steady between Austria and its largest trading partner, Germany. This is done by maintaining a differential of about 1 percent in favor of those with savings accounts or bonds in Austrian schillings rather than German marks. As a result, Austrian bonds are an attractive investment.

To keep Austrian arbitrators from taking advantage of the spread, the central bank operates a system of exchange controls. Foreigners, however, are exempt from those controls.

FOREIGN ADVANTAGE

Austrian residents are subject to much higher taxes than foreigners. When you open an Austrian bank account, you must prove that you are a foreigner—which you do by showing your passport. Unlike the situation in other banking havens, however, no one needs to write down the information in your identification papers to start up your account.

Once the bank knows you are a foreigner, you can devise another way to identify yourself. You can use a pseudonym, a number code, or a password if you open a securities account as well as a savings account. If you open only a savings account, you will have to use your name.

The account need not be in Austrian schillings. Most major currencies are acceptable. Austrian banks pay rates close to those of the wholesale rates offered by Euromarkets on relatively modest amounts on deposit in most major currencies. You may open an account with any amount. (There is no minimum at all).

BUYING STOCKS AND BONDS

Austria has had one of the best-performing stock markets in the world in recent years. As the likeliest beneficiary from the crumbling of the Iron Curtain, it will probably continue to boom.

Nonresidents are not subject to restrictions on securities purchases. You can buy an unlimited amount of Austrian and foreign bonds and stocks on condition that the money used is either foreign currency or "free schillings" (Austrian currency outside the exchange-control system). When these securities are sold, the proceeds can be exported and freely converted. Securities bought in Austria can be sent or taken abroad without restrictions.

However, there is (as there must be) a way for the Austrian tax authorities to make money out of their banking haven status. Bank account interest in schillings is taxed at 1 percent (of the amount paid you, not a cut in the interest of 1 percent). If the bank account is in a foreign currency, there is no tax. Interest from investments with Austrian banks in non-bearer form (such as certificates of deposit) are not subject to the tax. Neither are foreigners subject to taxation in Austria on bond interest.

Interest from convertible bonds, however, is subject to withholding at 20 percent; 20 percent withholding also is withheld at the source on share dividends. Shares in Austrian companies are subject to a local Austrian capital-gains tax when they are sold, also now 20 percent. The capital-gains tax applies to bonus shares, dividend certificates, bonus bonds, and other instruments that might be used in place of straight dividends to avoid the tax on dividends. The capital-gains tax is paid by the company or body making the payment. So the foreigner doesn't have to do anything to meet Austrian tax liability.

U.S. TAX TREATY

Of course, you still are subject to capital-gains tax in your own country on the capital gain deducted at the source in Austria. This hardship is eased by the existence of a U.S. double-taxation treaty with Austria. If you file with the IRS under the double-taxation law, your Austrian tax will be partly repaid, so the Austrian bite is only 10 percent on capital gains.

The other 10 percent can offset part of the U.S. capital-gains tax to which you would ordinarily be subject. Of course, when you file to get relief for capital-gains tax, you are telling the IRS that you may have had dividends or bond interest in previous reporting periods.

Because of the absence of laws on insider trading and the fact that withholding on dividends applies only to Austrian (not foreign) shares, Austria can be used to operate in foreign stock markets. If the recipient is an Austrian bank account, U.S. stock dividends and bond interest are subject to withholding at the source. Only if you file for a tax refund with the IRS and arrange to pay U.S. taxes on the dividends or interest can you get back the withholding tax.

STATE-OWNED BANKS

Most of the large Austrian banks are ones in which the state is the majority stockholder, which some people may think is a reason to avoid them. The Austrian banks were nationalized along with much of the country's heavy industry to protect their assets from the Russians during the four-power occupation of the country after World War II. There is, therefore, nothing ideological about Austrian bank nationalization.

Because they are government owned, Austrian banks have extremely low capital and equity. They typically control huge blocks of Austrian industry, however. This is a result both of the use of banks as holding companies (a tradition also in Germany) and of the need to protect industrial plants and equipment from being shipped to the Soviet Union during the occupation.

The lack of equity and the relatively low profitability may worry foreign depositors, particularly when they compare Austrian banks to Swiss banks. Mitigating the potential riskiness of Austrian banks is the fact that most of the loans they carry went to Austrian industrial holdings in their groups, rather than to foreign countries (as with large U.S. banks). Also, the Austrian government has a history of providing capital to large banks when the needs of the companies they control have created a potential problem. There is no reason to avoid Austrian-owned banks.

SELECTED BANKS IN AUSTRIA

- Creditanstalt Bankverein, Schottengasse 6-8, 1010-Vienna; tel. (43-1) 531310; fax (43-1) 533-4268
- Raiffeisen Zentralbank, Herrengasse 1, 1010-Vienna; tel. (43-1) 717070
- Girozentrale, Schubertring 5, 1010-Vienna; tel. (431) 711940; fax (43-1) 713-1806
- Laenderbank, Am Hof 2, 1010-Vienna; tel. (43-1) 531240; fax (43-1) 531-24155
- Zentralsparkasse, Fordere Zollamtstrasse 13, 1030-Vienna; tel. (43-1) 711-910
- Royal Trust Bank-Austria, Rathausstrasse 20, P.O. Box 306, 1011-Vienna, Austria; tel. (43-1) 43-6161; fax (43-1) 42-8142

CHAPTER 15

THE USE OF TAX HAVENS

This book is primarily aimed at using offshore secrecy havens as safe places to maintain your cash and passive investments, such as stocks and mutual funds. If you have an active business, you may have other uses for offshore tax havens.

Tax havens are one of the most important subjects for an international entrepreneur, yet few understand and use them properly. One group discounts them as mere hiding holes for dirty money, which is not a legitimate use for tax havens. Others think they are only for banking money after you have made it. Neither is true.

Money grows much faster if a tax haven is part of your business planning, and almost any international business has an opportunity to use tax havens. It is the purely domestic business, confined to one country, that cannot benefit from the international fiscal loopholes. Switzerland is a major financial center, but not generally a tax haven.

Simply stated, a tax haven is any country whose laws, regulations, traditions, and, in some cases, treaty arrangements make it possible for one to reduce his overall tax burden. This general definition, however, covers many types of tax havens, and it is important that you understand their differences.

NO-TAX HAVENS

These are countries that have no income, capital gains, or wealth (capital) taxes, and in which you can incorporate and/or form a trust. The governments of these countries do earn some revenue from corporations; "no-tax" means that what you pay is independent of income derived through a company. These states may impose small fees on documents of incorporation, a small charge on the value of corporate shares, annual registration fees, etc. Primary examples are Bermuda, Bahamas, and the Cayman Islands.

NO-TAX-ON-FOREIGN-INCOME HAVENS

These countries do impose income taxes, both on individuals and corporations, but only on locally derived income. They exempt from tax any income earned from foreign sources that involve no local business activities apart from simple "housekeeping" matters. For example, in such a haven there is often no tax on income derived from export of local manufactured goods.

The no-tax-on-foreign-income havens break down into two groups. There are those that allow a corporation to do business both internally and externally, taxing only the income coming from internal sources, and those that require a company to decide at the time of incorporation whether it will be one allowed to do local business with the consequent tax liabilities or one permitted to do only foreign business and thus be exempt from taxation. Primary examples in these two subcategories are Panama, Liberia, Jersey, Guernsey, Isle of Man, and Gibraltar.

LOW-TAX HAVENS

These are countries that impose at least a little tax on all corporate income, wherever earned. However, most have double-taxation agreements with many of the high-tax coun-

The Use of Tax Havens

tries that may reduce the withholding tax imposed on income derived from the high-tax countries by local corporations. Cyprus is a primary example. The British Virgin Islands is another, but it no longer has a tax treaty with the United States. Thus, a 2- to 5-percent tax paid to the haven eliminates or reduces the taxes to the high-tax country.

SPECIAL TAX HAVENS

These are countries that impose all or most of the usual taxes, but either allow special concessions to special types of companies (such as a total exemption from tax on shipping companies or movie production companies) or allow very special types of corporate organization, such as the flexible corporate arrangements offered by Liechtenstein. The Netherlands and Austria are particularly good examples of this.

To understand the precise role of tax havens, it is important for you to distinguish two basic sorts of income: 1) return on labor and 2) return on capital.

The first kind of return is what you get from your work: salary, wages, fees for professional services, etc. The second kind of return relates, basically, to the return from your investments: dividends on shares of stock; interest on bank deposits, loans, and bonds; rental income; royalties on patents. It is the second kind of income, income from an investment portfolio, that tax havens are useful for. Forming a corporation or trust in a tax haven can make the second form of income totally tax free or taxed so low that you will hardly notice. Certain types of businesses can be effectively based in a tax haven. If you publish a newsletter, for example, you might be able to set up the entire operation in a totally tax-free country such as the Bahamas or the Cayman Islands. If your income comes from copyright royalties, perhaps on the computer program you invented, the Netherlands is famed as a base for sheltering royalty income.

Tax havens are a very complex subject, but the hours you spend studying their use will probably pay you more per hour than the hours you spend directly earning an income—an unfortunate commentary on the confiscatory taxation policies of most governments.

For the best detailed information on tax havens, order *The Tax Haven Report* from Scope International Ltd., 62 Murray Road, Waterlooville, Hants., PO8 9JL, United Kingdom. The price is $125, including airmail postage worldwide, and VISA or MasterCard is accepted. If you want it by slower surface mail, the price is $100. The company will send a free catalog upon request.

Another source of information is Eden Press, which publishes a series of special reports on different havens and techniques by which Americans can use them. You can obtain its catalog free by writing to P.O. Box 8410, Fountain Valley, CA 92728.

If you want to gain a good understanding of how the government views tax havens, University Microfilms International, through its Books on Demand program, is now making available *Tax Havens and Their Uses by United States Taxpayers* by Richard Gordon. Frequently referred to as "The Gordon Report," this 1981 U.S. Treasury Department study was prepared at the request of Congress and gives considerable detail on and examples of the uses of tax havens. It is available from University Microfilms for $67.30 softbound or $73.30 hardbound. Out of print for more than a decade, it still provides useful information to anyone interested in tax havens. Copies can be ordered through booksellers or directly from University Microfilms International, 300 North Zeeb Road, Ann Arbor, Michigan 48106-1346; telephone 800-521-0600 or 313-761-4700. The UMI catalog number for the book is AU00435, and UMI accepts Visa or MasterCard.

Just stop and think for a moment how much faster your money can grow if you are not paying out an average of 40 percent to a taxing government somewhere.

CHAPTER 16 THE MONEY LAUNDRY UNDER ATTACK

Officials of the U.S. Drug Enforcement Agency are trying to get bank authorities in other countries to cooperate in a new scheme to collect information on senders and recipients of bank transfers. The idea is to prevent money laundering, which is the movement of the proceeds of crime into legitimate banking circuits through a foreign account that cannot be tracked.

When profits from the drug trade are used to buy more drugs, there is no need to involve legitimate banking circuits or to make wire transfers; cash is an acceptable mode of payment. It is also the way drug lords acquire cars, yachts, gold chains, art, and even real estate.

When the criminals have made so much money that they can no longer spend it or reinvest it in the drug business, however, they want to be able to buy stocks and bonds, life insurance, and legitimate businesses. For this they need bank accounts, checks, and bank drafts. You cannot deposit large amounts of cash into a U.S. bank without a record's being kept, so these criminals use foreign banks. The DEA seems to think that wire transfers are also being used and is, with embarrassing simplemindedness, trying to track such transfers.

The fight against drug dealing seems to entail trying to collect all information about movements of funds between the United States and overseas accounts. Of course, this information yields more than just what American criminals are up to.

Data on wire transfers could determine which Americans hold overseas accounts to check on whether they are reporting their existence (as is required by law if $10,000 or more is held abroad). This same information could be used to check up on American holdings abroad to enforce tax laws, inheritance laws, bankruptcy rulings, or the results of malpractice suits.

U.S. officials are focusing attention on private banking, which means large transactions on behalf of wealthy individuals internationally. The key to the U.S. effort to crack down on money laundering is the Anti-Drug-Abuse Act, which requires that the U.S. Treasury negotiate with other countries to establish financial-information-exchange agreements and encourage them to adopt bank reporting rules for U.S. currency transactions or ones originating in the United States. If the Treasury reports that a country is not negotiating in good faith, the president is required to deny banks of that country access to the U.S. payments system.

In addition, at the 1989 economic summit of the industrialized democracies, world leaders pledged cooperation to fight international movement of drug money. The Group of Seven (G7) countries (the United States, Britain, Japan, France, West Germany, Italy, and Canada) subsequently held meetings about how to proceed on this. Two G7 countries, Britain and Canada, are tightening their own laws on money laundering.

In the Bank for International Settlements, which is the central bank for central banks, the U.S. Federal Reserve in January 1989 won agreement from the governors of central banks of the Group of 10 (G10) countries to make it harder for people to deposit cash in banks in their jurisdictions. This is called the Basel Statement. (The Group of 10 consists of the United States, Britain, Canada, Japan, France, West Germany, Italy, Sweden, Belgium, and the Netherlands. Switzerland, which used to be an observer, is

The Money Laundry under Attack   143

now a full member, so the G10 is actually made up of 11 countries.) The Basel Statement marks a major departure for G10 supervision, which hitherto involved no international exchanges between supervisors on matters regarding details of individual depositors. Hitherto, the G10 had followed the so-called Cooke Principles (defined in 1983 by a committee headed by Peter Cooke, chief banking supervisor of the Bank of England), which specifically provided for recognition of banking secrecy. Now central banks will exchange information on individuals any central bank thinks are involved in money laundering. Bank secrecy does not apply in these cases.

The Anti-Drug-Abuse Act was passed by a Congress facing election pressure to get tough on drug dealers. The law tightened currency-transaction reporting rules for financial institutions and gave the Treasury power to demand additional information in some cases. This may include reports on transactions smaller than $10,000 for any 60-day period, which can be indefinitely extended. The bank will have to provide the name, birthdate, and Social Security number of each customer. Subsequent laws have done things like require reporting of money orders over $3,000 and reporting of cash receipts by car dealers, boat dealers, and other businesses. Furthermore, the bank is not allowed to tell customers why this information is being requested. A new $15 million data base center has been created by the U.S. Treasury to deal with the data. The Financial Crimes Enforcement Network (Fincen) will collect banking and personal data on cash movements among all financial institutions in the country and details of all wire transfers and all transactions involving sums in excess of $10,000.

Furthermore, banks are required to report "suspicious activity" even if large currency transactions are not involved. For example, the banks must use their judgment in reporting large increases in activity or a host of foreign transfers right under the $10,000 limit.

It is expected that the fine-tooth-comb reporting rules will target areas suspected of drug dealing, such as New York and Los Angeles, as well as areas where drug smuggling is believed to take place, such as Florida, Arizona, and Texas. Funds originating in target areas are more likely to be reported upon.

In theory, the controls are on cash deposits. There is a likelihood that banks will also want to keep track of large cash withdrawals. These too are liable to be considered suspicious. If you want to deal in cash, you should consider moving your account to an area not subject to this kind of scrutiny. We suggest Ohio or North Carolina. Also, remember that very little record is kept of cash withdrawals made through automatic teller machines or by using credit cards.

Thus far, most foreign bank authorities have resisted the effort to set up a generalized system for reporting transfers originating in the United States or deposits of cash above a certain size. What they are insisting on is a specific request from U.S. authorities about funds originating in the account of someone who is under suspicion and proof that a court order has been issued in the United States to subpoena such information for good cause.

In fact, some bank specialists think the new surveillance is not intended merely to track drug transactions. The Treasury is also the parent of the IRS and in charge of administering reporting requirements on overseas bank accounts held by Americans. So the motive may be to make money movements harder and more costly. It can be argued that such rules are intended to dissuade residents of the United States from moving their funds overseas even for legitimate purposes. Although the United States does not have exchange controls, it does have an increasingly onerous set of reporting rules. And lest we suffer from short memories, it is only recently that American laws were changed to permit investments in gold and foreign securities. During President Lyndon Johnson's administration in the 1960s we even were threatened with "temporary emergency" exchange controls on foreign travel.

THE SECURITIES AND EXCHANGE COMMISSION

The Securities and Exchange Commission is not any more mindful of the borders of the United States than is the Treasury. Of course, it too likes to collect data, and that is the main focus of its extraterritorial push through the newly created Office of International Affairs. The SEC has agreements with Britain, Switzerland, Japan, three Canadian provinces, Brazil, the Netherlands, and France. These try to ensure the "transparency and security" of international markets.

Transparency means that information should be available about companies and trading; security means that investors are protected against fraud, insider trading, and manipulation. In theory, this is a good idea. In practice, however, the Europeans are already having second thoughts.

The Dutch have one of the oldest stock markets in the business, and they have a very long relationship with U.S. markets. The first American bonds issued outside the country were sold during the American Revolution to Dutch investors. Several Dutch companies, notably Philips (Norelco in the United States) and Shell, actually have their shares directly listed by the New York Stock Exchange.

What is worrying to the Dutch is that the SEC is now demanding documentation and reporting from these companies in excess of what the Dutch themselves require. (The Amsterdam stock exchange, "Beurs," is self-regulated, and there is no equivalent of the SEC at all.) It is thus far asking for this information politely.

ENFORCING U.S. COURT ORDERS ABROAD

The Europeans have noticed that the SEC wants to have a U.S. court order work in another country. Some years ago, a grand jury in Miami ordered a Bahamian branch of the Bank of Nova Scotia to hand over bank statements of a defendant accused of evading payments to the IRS. It is against Bahamian criminal law for a bank to disclose information about a customer without his consent, and, in this case, the customer did not consent. Unfortunately, the Bank of Nova Scotia had a branch, assets, and staff in Miami, subject to sequestration and possible imprisonment. So the order was complied with after it had fought this outcome right up to the U.S. Supreme Court (1983).

Compulsory Waiver

In the past decade, the courts allowed something called a "compulsory waiver." Because most foreign laws contain a provision on bank confidentiality, the SEC started using subpoenas to bring parties before a court. Then the court would order that they must consent to disclosure of their affairs. If consent was not given, they could be imprisoned indefinitely for contempt of court.

This procedure was used regardless of the Fifth Amendment, which provides that no person shall be compelled to be a witness against himself. The U.S. Supreme Court in the grand jury investigation (Doe v. U.S.—"Doe II") ruled in favor of the SEC. In effect, the ruling concluded that no Fifth Amendment violation existed because producing bank records was not "evidentiary"—meaning that the individual is not being asked to testify against himself in violation of the Fifth Amendment.

Consent May Not Mean Consent

Consent given in response to the threat of indefinite imprisonment hardly sounds like consent, which is defined as "voluntary agreement" by most dictionaries. The issue came up again in SEC v. Wang and Lee in New York's Second Court of Appeals. The SEC was investigating alleged insider trading and trying to recover vast sums of illegal profits. The agency got New York District Court orders freezing Lee's assets on June 27, 1988, which purported to be effective worldwide. These orders prohibited any financial institutions holding the assets of Lee and/or 35 other named individuals (said to be his accomplices) from allowing these customers to withdraw or deal with the money said to have been gained through insider trading.

The bank affected was Standard Chartered, which operates a branch in New York and which had deposits totaling $12.5 million from Lee and his various parties in Hong Kong. Ten days later, Lee's lawyers in the crown colony demanded payment of all money in the accounts in question. Disobeying the New York court order made the bank liable to sequestration of its assets there, imprisonment of its staff for contempt of court, and other harassment.

Meanwhile, the Hong Kong courts ruled that they did not regard the U.S. court order as valid. A series of further orders were slapped on Standard Chartered to convert all the deposits into U.S. dollars and pay the total to the New York court.

Diplomatic Protest

The British government filed a diplomatic note of protest in Washington. The British Foreign Office, the Bank of England, and the British Department of Trade and Industry tried to protect the bank by filing amicus curiae briefs in the appeal. The New York Clearing House Association, the Institute of International Bankers, and the New York Foreign Bankers Association filed other such briefs, which were subscribed to by the British Bankers Association, the Canadian Bankers Association, the Committee of London & Scottish Bankers, the Hong Kong Association of Banks, and other bodies.

The way the U.S. court had acted in issuing the orders—the British diplomats, government officers, and bank supervisors argued—was likely to lead to less respect for the law. The amicus brief said, "The nature of the concern is that conflicting orders of courts of different jurisdictions affecting the same parties and the same subject matter cannot both be obeyed, so that the law of the country, the order of whose court is not obeyed, must necessarily be weakened and brought into disrepute."

The brief also noted that there was no way the bank could fulfill its duty to its client under Hong Kong law and also meet the New York court orders. "In the case of a bank it would often be the case that it would have branches in both of the jurisdictions in question, and so would be subject on the one hand to civil liability and on the other hand procedures for monetary penalty and imprisonment of its staff for disobeying the order of the court."

Persecution of Innocent Bystanders

The amicus brief also pointed out that the staff members of the bank, innocent of any wrongdoing, were subject to imprisonment and penalties, which was unfair. It also noted that international comity (the rules of polite conduct between nations) was being violated by the New York court. "The difficulties of innocent third parties might be avoided and the comity of nations preserved if it was accepted that no such court would make orders with extraterritorial effect on parties against whom no substantive relief was sought, unless subject to the endorsement of the foreign court in question."

The final result was a standoff. In the end, the SEC agreed to an out-of-court settlement with Lee et al. Lee "voluntarily" agreed to transfer the funds to New York. Standard Chartered won a moral victory because its costs were provided for, and it avoided having to pay out the $12.5 million twice. But the District Court orders were not overruled, and no decision was made about their validity.

Contempt for the Law

One result of the ham-fisted behavior of the courts, the SEC, the DEA, and the Treasury has been that other countries often refuse to cooperate in cracking down on money laundering even when the indications of it are clearest. By taking a broadbrush approach, American regulators are clearly hoping to catch violators of U.S. tax and securities law who are not drug smugglers at all. By doing so, however, they are in fact making it easier for European banking centers, which want to ignore such efforts to do so.

In the Swiss Federal Banking Commission investigation of

the use of two Swiss banks by a pair of suspected Lebanese money launderers, the final report determined that no additional banking regulations were needed. The laundering operation, which ended in mid-1988, transformed a total of nearly $1 billion (SFr 1.4 billion) delivered in cash (bank note) form to the banks in Switzerland. It was turned into deposits in 300 banks outside Switzerland and into precious metals investment.

The Swiss simply decided to do nothing about their law (which one U.S. bank regulator called "as full of holes as their cheese") precisely because there was so much pressure from the United States to impose quantitative rules, which go against the Swiss grain. The Swiss, in common with other banking centers dedicated to secrecy, will reveal client account information if criminal charges have been brought. They are not prepared, however, to operate a reporting system based on amounts (i.e., telling an official about any transaction worth more than $10,000) as in the United States.

Italy, which has become a channel for "dirty money," is treading very cautiously. Although a Socialist politician, Rino Formica, has called for the lifting of Italian banking secrecy entirely, mainstream Italian officials point out that, in practice, Italian banks do not offer secrecy comparable to that offered over the border in Switzerland.

However, in parts of Italy, notably Sicily, cash is king, and one way to crack down on drug money may be to require that those dealing with their banks on a cash basis be identified. One proposal being considered by the Italian authorities is that in the future anyone undertaking a cash operation involving more than 10 million lire be required to identify himself. Ten million lire is $75,000, a rather considerable amount compared to the $10,000 used by American banking regulators. Thus far, the measure has not been enacted into law. Bluster and blunder by the DEA make it more remote.

Dr. Fritz Diwok of the Verband Oesterreichische Banken und Bankiers, a bankers' organization, had this to say about the DEA effort in a May 1990 interview in Private Banker-International (published in Dublin, Ireland): *"In common with other countries, we believe we cannot react when we receive a list of 1,000 Panamanian names, starting with the general and director of the airport, then their girlfriends, and then their relations, with no indication as to whether these people have committed a crime."*

The Future of Exchange Controls

In Western Europe exchange controls have been lifted completely in most countries. All EC members are required to permit free movement of funds within the EC. Some of the countries outside the EC still maintain some form of control, particularly Austria, Sweden, and Norway. Exchange controls also exist in most of the developing world and in the former East Bloc, where there are plans to lift them over time.

It would be ironic if the United States were to impose hindrances on the free flow of money just as other countries are coming around to a liberal position. Some of the recent measures taken by U.S. authorities in the supposed crackdown on insider trading and drug dealing come perilously close to introducing exchange controls on Americans.

CONCLUSION

"Banks have done more injury to the religion, morality, tranquility, prosperity, and even wealth of the nation than they can have done or ever will do good."

—John Adams, President, United States 1819

Confidence in American financial institutions continues to erode. A 1989 study by *American Banker* revealed that more than 30 percent of respondents said they had less faith in the system than in previous years.

Could the U.S. financial crisis of the 1990s result in the same kind of deflationary collapse that brought on the Great Depression of the 1930s? The answer is a clear yes—especially if the Federal Reserve miscalculates on the scale that it did 60 years ago. But the odds are against it.

Of course, the odds were probably against it in 1930 too. At any time, there are always some potential catastrophes waiting in the wings. Most never occur. The ones that beat the odds, however, are the ones that really clobber us.

That's why you should take reasonable precautions now to diversify your savings abroad. After all, taking steps to guard against the unexpected is what prudence is all about. Having read this far, you now know what to do. Go out and do it.

ABOUT THE AUTHOR

Adam Starchild is the author of more than a dozen books and hundreds of magazine articles, primarily on international business and finance. Four of his books are on tax havens. The most recent are *The Tax Haven Report,* published by Scope International (a British publisher) in 1993, and *Tax Havens for International Business*, published by Macmillan in Britain in 1994.